ADVANCE PRAISE FOR MILESTONES

"Life is a series of incremental steps. This book offers a great roadmap toward creating one that most can only dream."

Rob Angel, author, *Game Changer*, and founder of Pictionary

"When it comes to communication, I thought I had heard it all. Brandl has definitely proved me wrong. Simply great!"

Andrea Böhm, First Austrian Bank

"Absolutely relevant to practice and directly implementable."

Borries von Mueller, Global Head HR Fresenius Medical Care

"Peter's hands-on experience as an entrepreneur, commercial pilot, and communications expert make his advice so exciting."

Michael Baumann, Managing Director, MTU South Africa

"Simple, amazing insights for creating all that is possible."

Garth Watrous, CEO American Hat Makers

MILESTONES

PETER BRANDL

KATJA PORSCH

DR. GREG REID

Milestones

Peter Brandl, Katja Porsch, Dr. Greg Reid

Copyright © 2020

All rights reserved.

Joint Venture Publishing

Blue Sky R&D, LLC

ISBN: 978-1-7351657-0-7

TABLE OF CONTENTS

FOREWORD

There are milestones in life that create the legacies we leave behind. Some are the product of goals, while others are created by opportunities that present themselves during the course of our lifetime. These goals and opportunities are available to everyone; however, they often come with challenges and are, therefore, written off as unattainable dreams or wishes.

As you read through these pages, you will quickly realize that the most complex challenges have the most simplistic solutions. In this book, you'll meet Heidi and her mentors, John and Mia, who share the strategies that create awareness and progress toward her success and happiness. Like Heidi, when you apply them to your life and goals, you'll be rewarded with the success that has previously been beyond your reach.

Everyone has dreams and wishes. Let this book bring you closer to yours ... one milestone at a time.

Frank Shankwitz
Co-Founder, Make A Wish Foundation

Chapter One

THE FIRST STEP

Heidi had always known she wanted to be a businesswoman. When other children played house with their little dolls, Heidi chose another path, donning her mother's high heels and carrying around a briefcase. She pretended to make important phone calls and loved to wheel and deal, making business transactions with imaginary associates.

Now that she was an adult, the reality was much different. Yes, she was a businesswoman and had the college degree and education to be successful. But success always seemed to be in the distance, and try as she might, Heidi couldn't get any closer to it. She had spent several years gaining much-needed experience in corporate America, and she had learned a lot. Now, she found she was ready to climb the proverbial ladder or, better yet, branch off on her own and become an entrepreneur with her own company and brand. Unfortunately, neither of these things were happening, and Heidi was becoming frustrated, wondering if her opportunity would ever present itself.

Internally, Heidi felt a lot of conflict. She was an ambitious young woman who seemed to be going nowhere. Even her name was a source of conflict and contention with her—it was an old-fashioned German name, so much so that people rarely named their daughters Heidi anymore. To top it off, Heidi wasn't old fashioned at all—she was a go-getter, a modern woman with 21st century dreams of success and esteem. Her parents, however, named her Heidi because it was a family name, and they'd chosen their daughter to carry on the legacy. Her parents said it was a name that she should carry with pride, but she'd never felt like it really suited her.

Her parents also told her that success would take time. She understood that, but patience also wasn't one of her strongest traits. Besides, she'd heard of plenty of young entrepreneurs who had created phenomenal businesses in their 20s. Truth be told, her lack of patience was one reason she wasn't content at work. In her opinion, she didn't have enough responsibility and, therefore, she was bored. With no sign of a promotion in the near future, she dreaded the thought of putting in 20 or 30 years before she began to reap the rewards of her education. If she wanted to live her dream, it was beginning to look like she was going to have to make the move toward business ownership, rather than leaving her career at the mercy of someone else.

When she dared to dream, she allowed herself to envision the type of business she wanted to own. She had once heard that it was best to go into business doing something you are passionate about. She was passionate about business, and she had to admit that she didn't have any regular hobbies. However, one of the things she enjoyed doing was recreating her grandmother's recipes. Heidi's grandmother had grown up in Germany and brought with her a great knowledge of the foods, flavors, and cuisines. As a child, Heidi enjoyed spending time with her grandma, listening to her talk about her native country when she was cooking, while Heidi pretended to be a customer at her grandmother's "restaurant," which was actually a chair at the kitchen table that gave Heidi a firsthand view of her grandmother's culinary skills.

As a result, Heidi had grown to love authentic German food. Unfortunately, though, there weren't any restaurants in their area that offered such a menu, with a wide variety of choices. So whenever Heidi missed her grandparents or craved German cuisine, she pulled out her grandmother's recipe box. Over the years, she added her own touch to some of them and had become a cook that she hoped her grandmother would have been proud of.

These were the type of thoughts and memories that went through Heidi's mind at night, but come morning, she'd push them aside and get ready to go to the office. No, it wasn't anything like her childhood dream, but it was a paycheck and would have to do until another opportunity presented itself.

Mondays were always busy at work. At the beginning of the week, there was always a staff meeting, where they learned about their weekly goals and roles. On this day, Heidi was told the company was expecting one of their corporate sponsors at the end of the week, and she was expected to serve as his assistant while he was there. She didn't mind—it would be a change of pace that she actually looked forward to. Besides, she was an organizer at heart, and she knew her supervisor had chosen her because she would anticipate the executive's needs and have the necessary files and supplies necessary to make his visit a productive one.

Heidi had never personally met this individual; however, she had heard him speak at a company conference once. His presentation was so enjoyable that when he returned as a presenter the next year, she made sure she was in the audience. From her coworkers, she knew John was a highly successful corporate executive, and talk was that he was also very down to earth—a good-natured man who was willing to listen to people at all levels within the company. For that reason, he had a reputation for being well liked and respected. Heidi hoped so—during her college internship, she'd worked with a demanding boss who didn't appreciate his employees, and it was horrible.

Heidi spent the week getting everything organized. She hired a service to pick him up at the airport and set him up with a temporary office. She printed his daily schedule and placed it in the center of his desk, along with the contact information for every person he would be meeting with during his stay. She left no stone unturned and felt confident that she had anticipated everything he might need, right down to staples and paper clips.

On Friday morning, she was surprised when John, the executive, walked into her office to thank her. A distinguished looking man, he wore an impeccable suit and his dark hair was sprinkled with gray in a few strategic spots. His voice, though, was relaxed and friendly, and his tone was sincere.

"You must be Heidi," he said. "I just wanted to stop in and thank you for all the preparations you made for me. I really appreciate your effort."

"You're welcome," Heidi replied, with a smile. "I will be here and available if you need anything during the next week. I'm happy to help in any way I can."

John approached her several times, usually to ask a question about an employee. Who was that person? What was their job title? What department did they work in? He really did want to know about the people who worked for the company, and he listened intently as Heidi answered his questions with as much detail as she could.

At the end of the day, John asked her to stop in his office for a few minutes. When she arrived, he asked her to sit down and talk.

"Heidi, as you can tell, I've tried to learn about the people who work here. I know that a business is only as good as its employees—they are our greatest investment and our most valuable asset. I asked you to stop by because there is someone I didn't ask about yet."

"Who is that?" Heidi asked.

"You," he replied. "Tell me about yourself and your time here at the company."

"Well, I have been here for four years. As a matter of fact, I was hired right after I graduated from college," she said.

"And do you like what you do?" John asked.

Not sure how to respond, Heidi paused … just long enough that John caught the hesitation.

"I do like my job, sir," she answered. "But I believe I am ready for more responsibility. However, there aren't that many opportunities."

"Let me ask, if I can, what are your career goals?" he asked.

"I'd like to be a decision maker, someone like you. I've always wanted to be an executive, or even an entrepreneur," she admitted.

"I see. Heidi, if that's what you want, what's stopping you? You certainly seem qualified and capable. Why are you waiting for an opportunity to come your way, instead of going out and making it happen?"

"I guess I don't know what to do ... or how to go about it," Heidi replied.

"You want to change something, you want success, you want to make more out of your life? Many people want that. Many dream of the big position, the big house, the new car, the dream family, or the fat bank account. But only few achieve it. Do you think it's about opportunities? Coincidence? Fate? Luck?"

"I'm not sure," she said.

"The few who get those things decide things differently. They are not more talented, not more educated, and not more favored. They do things while others think, hesitate, and wait. They want it more than anything else in the world, and they have learned how to get what they want."

"Heidi, I know that it's difficult to get started. There are a lot of variables and concerns. I've found, though, that there are several reasons why people find it hard to take action and become successful. There is a fear of change. Sometimes, the environment around them advises against making major changes. Then, there is always the hesitance to give up the security of a current job. And let's not forget, it's not easy to do when you have no experience. Do any of those things sound familiar to you?"

"Yes," Heidi admitted. "To be honest, all of them do."

"I've found that people have to learn how success works. Success is a muscle, and it has to be trained. If you don't train, you lose."

"How do you train for success?" Heidi asked, perplexed.

"Well, Heidi, let me tell you a story. You see, I actually had to train for success. If I hadn't, I know I wouldn't be here today," John replied.

"What did you do?"

"It all started when I was a child. From the time I was old enough to talk, I developed a speech impediment—a stutter. Now, it wasn't just any stutter. It didn't happen only when I was excited. I stuttered every time I tried to talk. As you can imagine, when I got into school, some of the other kids made fun of me because of that stutter. Naturally, this made me very self-conscious, and the last thing I wanted to do was stand in front of class to give an oral book report or a speech," he explained.

"Really? I'd never guess. Your speech is perfect. Actually, you're an excellent speaker. I've attended two of your presentations and enjoyed every minute of them. Your voice is very pleasant to listen to, and you have a way of capturing the audience's attention," Heidi said.

"Well, thank you. But it wasn't always like that. There was a time when the mere thought of public speaking put me in panic mode. It was like a vicious cycle—I hated speaking because I stuttered, and the more anxious I became about stuttering and speaking, the more I stuttered. It seemed I wasn't suited for a career that required speaking in any way. Quite the opposite, I was more suited for a job where I could let a keyboard do the talking."

"What did you do about it?" Heidi asked.

"Well, thankfully, I had great parents and good teachers who all recognized that I needed professional help. My parents sent me to speech therapy, and some of my teachers recommended alternate projects and assignments that didn't require speaking in front of the class. But I have to tell you, Heidi, it took a long time before I was able to talk for any real length of time without stuttering, even occasionally. Speech therapy was critical to my success, but it took faith and persistence on my part. And practice—a lot of practice. I spent hours upon hours practicing reading out loud and talking in my bedroom, saying things over and over again until I found the right pace and rhythm so I wouldn't stutter. To be honest, to this day, I still catch myself stuttering from time to time. So to answer your question, that was part of my training for success. I had to learn, train, and practice how to talk and be comfortable when speaking in front of others."

"So, we all have challenges to overcome. For me, it was my stuttering. For you, it is definitely something different. But whatever your challenges are, there are some things you can do to overcome them. In fact, it is crucial that you master some of them."

"Let's take a look at several of the steps you can take. Step one: You have to be 100 percent clear about where you want to go and what you want to do. What drives you? What is your Why? Without a 'why,' you don't need a what or a how. Step two: you have to make a commitment—an inner obligation with yourself that you are going to do everything it takes and won't give up until you've achieved what you want. And the last step, Heidi, is you have to take the first step and get started. You cannot wait for opportunity to knock on your door—you have to go out and make it happen."

"That sounds easier said than done," Heidi replied.

"In some ways, it is. I had to have a good enough why to do the work to overcome my speech impediment. Then I really had to be committed to it—it had to be something I really, really wanted to do. Otherwise, I wouldn't give it my all. Last, I had to actually do it. I had to go to therapy, I had to practice and keep practicing, even if I wasn't seeing the progress I wanted as fast as I wanted. I learned that success doesn't happen overnight; it's a process, sometimes a lengthy one. But the process of training for success is a start and a good one. You see, opportunity is everywhere. People just don't recognize it. I tell you what, if you're willing, I'd like to help you train your success muscle and pursue your dreams. My speech deficit was only one example. I had many more obstacles and challenges to overcome. And I did overcome them. Now I enjoy helping others grow and prosper, whether it is here in our company or outside of it. I think you have a bright future ahead of you, Heidi, and if you're interested, I would be happy to give you advice and counsel along the way. If you are serious about creating success, I would be willing to be your mentor," John offered.

"Really? That would be great! How do we get started?" Heidi asked excitedly.

"Well, I think we already got started. Now, it's time for you to take that first step. Heidi, the only person who knows where you want to go and what you want to do is you. Figure that out, and I'll help you get there."

Chapter Two

START YOUR ENGINE

The weekend brought Heidi an opportunity to reflect on her dreams once again. Sunday was "family dinner," a weekly tradition when her family would all go back home and have dinner together, just like they did when she was a child. It was different now, though, because everyone pitched in and brought a dish. Heidi didn't mind at all. As often as she could, she'd make one of her grandmother's authentic German dishes, which everyone really appreciated. It made her feel good to watch her family enjoy her culinary skills, and to her, it was the best way to pay tribute to her grandmother and their time spent together in her kitchen.

On Sunday morning, she purchased the ingredients she needed for her contribution to the evening meal. She was planning to do a special dish she knew from her granny – pan-fired potato dumplings with gravy. To Heidi, this dish was special and fun—special because potato dumplings are a rather elaborate dish. Making them from scratch really takes time and effort. The process includes mashing boiled potatoes, grating rare potatoes, and then mixing them together and forming the dumplings. After a few more steps, she slowly boiled the dumplings. Because preparation took so much time, she usually made them only on Sundays, which made them special, not an everyday entrée. Even though it was time consuming, Heidi found it fun, mainly because pan-fried dumplings were made from leftovers. Whatever was left over from the Sunday meal was cut into slices, fried in a pan and served with a delicious gravy that was also left over from Sunday. Her grandma used to make them only for Heidi. After all the family ate and was gone, Heidi had everything she needed for a special lunch on Monday, prepared just for her by her grandmother. It brought a smile to her face whenever she thought about it.

On her way back from the grocery store, Heidi passed a food truck that advertised tacos, enchiladas, and burritos. But what really caught her eye was the fried ice cream. Feeling like she deserved a treat, she turned around and got in line. It was amazing, she thought, how these mobile restaurants attracted business. Not only were they convenient, but they were also much more affordable than a brick and mortar structure, with less upkeep and maintenance.

She sat on a bench and indulged in the creamy, cold ice cream. Fried and frozen were exact opposites, she thought, but they were also the perfect complement to each other. Before she knew it, her mind had drifted, and she was daydreaming about what items she would offer customers if she had a food truck that served authentic German food. How much fun would it be to prepare and sell her special family dishes, like her grandmother's pan-fried dumplings with gravy and original German sausages with sauerkraut. Oh, and wouldn't people love to try her delicious apple strudel! Authentic, made from scratch German food was certainly a rarity, but she just knew it would be a hit and people would love it as much as she did.

That's when it hit her that she actually liked the idea! It was intriguing. Cooking and German cuisine were things she was passionate about and enjoyed. And it was a business ... but was it what she really wanted to do with her career and her life?

Yes! No ... Maybe. She was confused. On one hand, she was still the same ambitious go-getter who dreamed of corporate board rooms and climbing the proverbial ladder to the top, where she would triumphantly break through that seemingly impenetrable glass ceiling. She didn't think she was ready to give that up just yet. On the other hand, the idea of doing what she enjoyed and being her own boss was appealing. But then again, like John had told her, the thought of forgoing the security of a regular paycheck was scary. In other words, if she failed, both of her dreams would be lost.

Maybe, she thought, it was something John would be willing to talk about with her. Maybe he could help her weigh the pros and cons and come to the right decision.

Still, while she was preparing the potato dumplings to take to her parents' house for dinner, she caught herself envisioning tweaks that she could make that would perfect the recipe and appeal to a wide audience. If she ever did explore a business of her own, she would need several signature dishes, but judging by her family's response, her German potato dumplings were one of their favorites.

The next day, she spoke with John and told him about her idea … and her doubts.

"I was hoping that you could help me decide which direction to take. Should I keep trying to climb the corporate ladder? Or should I give up on that dream and open my own business?"

John contemplated her question for just a moment before he responded.

"Heidi, I commend you for being able to identify another path you'd like to pursue. I can also understand your reluctance to give up on your current path. Who knows where it will take you? If you quit now, you might not ever know what could have been," he said.

"That's right! John, I'm afraid if I make the wrong choice, I'll lose out on both opportunities," she said.

"Heidi, let me tell you a story. Everyone has a dream. Sometimes it goes back years, and sometimes it comes to us without warning. Imagine that you visited a beautiful city and absolutely fell in love with the place. It brought you nothing but peace and happiness. From that moment, it was your dream that this would someday be your home. On that day, you proclaimed that this is where you are going to live for the rest of your life. But you didn't know how you were going to make it happen. You didn't have a job there or the money to buy a house in the area. The only thing you had was a dream. What would you do?"

"I don't know. That's a tough question. Obviously, I can't buy the house just yet ..." she answered.

"That is right. You cannot. But do you give up on the dream because you don't know if it will ever happen or if it does happen, how it will work out? Or do you start to take steps to make it happen, having faith that if you do, someday a nice house in the beautiful city you love will be yours?" John asked.

"Heidi, you don't have to answer that. Just know that when it comes to dreams, especially those that take time, there are two types of dreamers—rockets and Yugos. The rockets never let their dream die. They don't let doubt set in. They take action to make it happen, even if it is just small steps. They are constantly on the move, progressing in some way toward their dream, even if they don't have all the answers."

"The Yugo, on the other hand, is an extreme realist who doesn't believe it is realistic to put in the time and effort for something if they don't have all the answers and know the outcome before they begin. They move slowly, if they even bother to take action at all," he explained.

"So you're saying I should be a rocket and dive in with both feet? Are you saying I should go ahead and make this major career change, even if I don't know how I'll get it done or how it is supposed to work?"

"Not at all. What I am I saying, Heidi, is that there is not 'one' reality. Take you and me. We are two different personalities. A man and a woman. I'm a few years older than you. We have two different educational backgrounds, and we've had different experiences in our lives. Don't you think we have a different view on the same things sometimes? And based on our experiences and these different views we have, wouldn't you agree that we have a different perception about what is around us? At the same time, we believe in what we perceive and make it 'our reality.' Like I said, Heidi, there is no 'one' reality. It simply does not exist. Reality to you is what *you* believe in. The good news is that you can create new realities with your dreams. A rocket has grand dreams—to soar to the moon! A Yugo, however, is struggling just to get his engine started and might even have a faulty starter. Dreams are the motor of our lives; a life without dreams is like a car with a damaged engine. It will never get you where you want to go," he said.

"Okay, so what do you recommend I do?" Heidi pleaded.

"First, ask yourself why you have to do either one thing or the other. You don't have to quit this dream to pursue an opportunity for another," he said.

"You mean to do both? Is that realistic?" she asked.

"I'm not saying you need to go out and buy a food truck tonight," he laughed. "But you don't have to wait to start your engine. You can do that today and tomorrow and every day until you feel the time is right. You can explore both careers until you see which one is most fulfilling to you. But if you start asking yourself if it's realistic, you will be like a Yugo and extinguish your dream."

"Oh, I get it. I don't need to make major changes right now. You're saying I can use this time wisely and start making plans and taking action so that one day, when I'm ready, I can open a food truck, even if it's only a weekend gig?"

"Yes. But don't let doubt and uncertainties get in your way, or at least use them wisely. Consider what they want to tell you but then remove them out of your mind. Otherwise, they'll make your engine choke and sputter and eventually you will lose steam. I can assure you if that happens, you won't get very far, and discouragement will kill your dream just like that," John said, snapping his fingers together.

"Interesting. What's the best thing I can do to start my engine? What do I have to do to get started?" Heidi asked.

"The first and most important thing you can do is to believe and don't ask yourself: how is that supposed to work? If you start to have doubts, turn to trust and ask yourself: Why not?" John advised.

"Why can't I do that …," she repeated. "Yes, why not? Why not me? I can do this! I know I don't know anything about the food business, but I can learn. Why not?" Heidi repeated, smiling.

"Experience isn't everything. Sometimes it's that burning desire, that relentless drive that will take us further than what we know or have learned. As a matter of fact, Heidi, experience can be a deterrent in the pursuit of what we want. Experiences can be like obstacles that prevent us from getting from one place to another. And we've all had plenty of experiences to tap into. Some good, some bad. But they are in the past, and I want you to remember that you'll always need to be looking ahead toward the future. To do that, you have to let go of old experiences; they prevent the making of new ones."

"John, for the first time in a couple years, I can actually say I'm excited about the future. I'm inspired to stop spinning my wheels and start doing something! It's like new life has been breathed into me," Heidi said. "And I owe it to you. Before I talked to you, I truly believed that I had to choose one career over another, but now I can see that I don't have to give up on one dream to have another. How can I thank you?"

"Hmm, well, if you really want to thank me, follow my advice. I do have your best interests at heart, and I do have the knowledge you need to get started on the right foot," John answered.

"Oh, I most certainly will follow your advice! And I'll keep you updated on my progress, too," Heidi promised.

"Great, but there is one more thing you can do for me, Heidi," John said.

"What's that?" she eagerly asked.

"Can you bring me some of those potato dumplings of yours? I'd love to be your first taste tester," he said.

"You bet I will," she laughed. "But first, I have to finish writing this report … the corporate ladder is still waiting, too."

Chapter Three

BE THE PILOT OF YOUR LIFE, NOT THE PASSENGER

Heidi was really motivated to make things happen in her life. When she was at work, she was committed to being attentive and focused, always looking forward toward the future she wanted within the company. While she hadn't identified the perfect opportunity to climb the ladder just yet, she knew that it would come. Her job was to be ready when it arrived.

In the meantime, her off hours were filled with research and education. She researched everything she could find about owning a food business. When she was out in the city, she kept her eyes open, looking for food trucks at every turn. When one caught her eye, she took note of everything—the signage, advertisement, its overall appearance, and even how many customers were in line. She noted its location—was it on a busy street, near a corner, in a parking lot? She even began to frequent the local farmer's market every week so she could partake in their wares and take notice of what people were spending their money on.

It was an education of observation. She wanted to be well informed about the industry, but even more, she needed to be highly informed about the competition. Thankfully, she found she was right—nowhere did she see a single vendor who sold German food and cuisine.

Actually, Heidi felt good. John was right—this was something she could do. She had the talent, thanks to her grandmother, but most important, she now had the focus and the motivation to make it happen. Taking action was the first step.

However, when she discovered the cost of a new food truck, her mouth almost hit the floor. She didn't have that kind of money, and there was no way she could come up with it, short of becoming quite wealthy in a short period of time. Was this the end? Heidi was so disappointed because all of her dreams suddenly seemed impossible. She really did not see any way she was going to be able to make things happen. There was just too much standing between her and the success she wanted to achieve.

Her best friend, Emily, agreed. Emily had been one of the first people she had dared to share her idea with … and she'd also been the first person to knock that dream down.

"You're kidding, right?" Emily asked with a laugh.

"No, I'm not. I really want to do this," Heidi answered, a little hurt by her friend's easy dismissal of something that meant so much to her.

"But why, Heidi? You've got everything you need! You're young, you've got a really good job. I mean, the world's at your feet—and you want to own a *food truck?* Who wants to do that? Do yourself a favor and stick with your job. At least there, you can get somewhere in life," Emily urged.

"But I'm not really fulfilled at work. I'm not doing what I really want to do, and who knows, Em, it could be years before I can climb up in the company. I have to be realistic. It might never happen," Heidi replied.

"I just can't believe that you're even thinking about throwing all that away, though! There are so many who would be jealous of you. And besides, do you have any idea how to cook professionally?" she asked.

"Uh, no, but I'm willing to learn—to train so I can," Heidi answered.

"Do you have the money to start your own business? Gee, Heidi, do you even know anything about running your own business? Experienced business owners fail every single day, and they know what they're doing!" Emily exclaimed. "If they can fail, what makes you think that you could do it?"

"I know. But I really think I can …"

Before Heidi finished, Emily interrupted. "And German food? Kraut and beer, who wants that? Where are you going to find customers? Maybe I wouldn't be so skeptical if you said you wanted to serve burgers or hot dogs or tacos, but sauerkraut? Yuck! Heidi, I love you, but I think you've lost your mind!"

By now, Emily had shot down Heidi's dream so much she was starting to believe that it really was a bad idea. As she silently listened to her friend bash her new dream, she became more and more discouraged. But she wasn't ready to give the dream up entirely, at least not until she factored in the cost of a food truck.

That's when she realized that Emily was probably right. Who was she kidding, thinking she could actually jump in and start her own business? Shaking her head, she wondered if Emily had actually done her a favor and was trying to save her from making a big mistake.

Initially, she was surprised that she had already become so invested in her vision. The sudden obstacles she was experiencing weighed heavily on her mind, and instead of the inspiration and excitement she had initially felt, the only thing she felt now was disappointment and frustration. All of the old feelings came rushing back, along with Emily's words. Maybe I'm not good enough. Is this even possible? What made me even think I could do this?

The more she thought about it, the more obstacles came to her mind and the farther her plans moved away from reality. She even wished she'd never gotten her hopes up. In doing so, she felt even more discouraged than she had before.

That made her upset with John. He had to have known that it was going to be difficult, even impossible, for her to go out and start a new business. She had zero experience as an entrepreneur, no equipment, and he had to have known she wasn't rich. How could he encourage her to pursue something that was obviously impossible? How could he get her hopes up, knowing that they were going to be shot down? Heidi shook her head. Not only was she disappointed in John, she was also angry with him. But she was also a little scared. The next time she met with him, she had no idea what would happen. What would she say to him? What would he say? Was there any way they could get past this and continue with their relationship? There were so many unanswered questions and feelings to deal with that she felt overwhelmed.

Heidi needed a little time to recover from this shock. Luckily for her, it was the weekend, so she had time to think about everything and digest what happened. She also knew that she had to face John on Monday, when they would normally meet.

Throughout the weekend, she continued to suffer from feelings of self-doubt and disappointment. Occasionally, though, she would dare to hope that maybe there was still some hope. After all, John had shared some good ideas with her, and he had given her a new perspective. Maybe, just maybe, he might have a perspective that she hadn't contemplated. Maybe he could see an option that she wasn't aware of. More than once in the last weeks since she'd met him, she was surprised with the options that suddenly came up or he showed her. She understood that sometimes when one is right in the middle of a problem, it is easy to get stuck and become blind to the alternatives and options that exist. She also learned that these are the precise types of situations where a mentor really can help. Maybe again, he'd have new ideas.

One minute, she had little faith in John, and then the next moment, she found herself relying on him for advice. "That's what a mentor is for," she said to herself. "A mentor can help you to find a way when you are lost. Right now, I'm about as lost as I can be." And by changing the words she spoke to herself, she realized that her thoughts also changed. And the more her thoughts changed, the more confident she became.

Her thoughts wavered between disappointment and possibility. One minute, she was consumed by Emily's obvious doubt in her ability, and the next, she found herself daydreaming about actually being successful. These were the types of thoughts that consumed her for the rest of the weekend. But by Sunday evening, there was a shift in her thinking, and she found that her fear was subsiding. Emily's words weren't so fresh, raw, and hurtful. And any doubt she'd had about John and his advice was dissipating. She wasn't angry with him any longer. On the contrary, she was actually looking forward to seeing John. She couldn't wait to tell him all about her challenges and get some new and fresh insight and ideas.

She took that excitement with her when she walked into their meeting. When she told John about the challenges that had presented themselves and how devastated she'd been, his reaction was of absolutely no surprise to her. Instead of focusing on what went wrong, he shifted the conversation in another direction.

"Heidi, this is about *your* life and *your* dreams. Are you going to be the pilot of your success or the passenger?" he asked.

"I guess the pilot—why?" she asked.

"Well, it seems to me that you were letting your friend, Emily, be the pilot and you let her tell you exactly what direction you were going to go in. You sat there and, like a good little passenger, you let her fly your dream straight into the ground as she fed your mind with negativity and self-doubt. Am I right?" John asked.

"Well, yes—in a way, but she did have some valid points. I can see where she was coming from, and maybe she's right …"

"And maybe she's not," John interrupted. "I will tell you one thing I know, though. If you ever want to succeed at anything, the best way to make sure you *don't* is to let other people stomp on your dreams and bring them down."

"Heidi, while you might think a brand new, shiny food truck is your best and only option, maybe that has to wait if it is not something you can do right now. Step back and think about what you *can* do," he said.

"Well, I guess I could use my savings as a down payment. Or maybe I can get a loan," she answered.

"Don't forget the opportunities and options you cannot see. There are always other options. But, unfortunately, these options hide themselves, so we can't see them on first sight. For example, why can't you purchase a used food truck and convert it to meet your needs? Or, if all else fails, there's always the option to find a partner who is willing to invest in your business," he mentioned.

A partner? Hmmm, that was a thought Heidi hadn't entertained. But who could she ask? Her father? He didn't have any real business experience, and although he was a great food connoisseur, he wasn't very gifted in the kitchen. The other possibilities that came to mind were people who she was certain didn't have the funds or the interest.

That left her with John's other possibility—buying a used food truck.

She got online and looked at classified ads and business ads. Maybe somebody was selling a food truck, or maybe there was someone out there who wanted to sell their entire business. That could open up quite a few more technical issues, but she didn't want to totally eliminate the option, not just yet, anyway.

A month passed before she spotted an opportunity in the local newspaper. Food truck for sale, all equipment included. To inquire, call Jose.

Grabbing a pen and paper, she quickly called the number listed.

"Hi, I'm calling about the food truck for sale. Is it still available?"

"Yes, it is. It's five years old and in good shape. I installed everything myself and I know it works," Jose answered.

During their conversation, Heidi learned that Jose had been a taco vendor and had used the food truck at different functions and events around the city. However, he indicated that taco trucks were now a dime a dozen and he felt it was time to turn his interests and business elsewhere. Figuring his loss was her gain, Heidi excitedly made an appointment to look at the food truck the next day.

When she arrived, she found Jose was right. The food truck and the equipment were in good shape. She'd have to change the signage, of course, but overall, she was impressed with what she saw. She was also surprised to find that Jose was willing to negotiate, and they came to an amicable agreement on the selling price.

Writing a check for the down payment, the only thing left for Heidi to do was to get a loan to cover the balance.

That's where she hit a brick wall.

Her bank informed her that she would need a business loan, not a personal loan. But there was a problem, she didn't actually have a business yet ...

Feeling a sense of urgency, Heidi picked up the phone and called John.

"It's like a catch-22, John. I can't get a loan because I don't have a business, and I can't have a business because I need a food truck and can't get a loan to buy it," she complained.

"Welcome to reality, Heidi," John said. "Believe me, in the business world, especially when you are a business owner, there will be obstacles that threaten your progress. But before we explore your options, let's address your attitude. Obstacles will present themselves, and one of the biggest challenges people face is not letting that first obstacle cause you to give up."

"But what if it seems impossible?" she asked.

"For centuries, people have given up on their dreams because they believe they're not possible. The people who are successful, however, know that this is the time when they absolutely must dig their heels in deeper and remain committed. It's easy to give up and quit, but they want success bad enough that they're willing to do what it takes to make it happen," John answered.

"Heidi, there is a lesson to be learned here, and it is an important one: How you deal with resistance will determine whether you continue … and how successful you will be. You can be the passenger on this journey and say that you don't have any control over what will happen. That transfers the blame for failure to someone else, so it's a protective mechanism. Or, if you're like me and those who've grown to enjoy success, you'll be the pilot on your journey. That gives you control over what happens. You get to fly your own aircraft and determine where it ends up."

"John, what do you suggest I do?"

"Before you make any moves or decisions, you have to learn how to deal with resistance—the obstacles that can and will come your way. I call them 'whams' because they seem to come out of nowhere and catch you by surprise."

"Yes, that's exactly how it feels. I know I didn't expect it!" Heidi exclaimed. "So you've experienced these whams, too—what did you do?"

"Well, right now, you have received your first no. I have had a successful career, but it wasn't without my share of obstacles. My success depends on being able to communicate with people. In order to lead others and influence them, I have had to overcome many obstacles, some when I was a young boy. It took time and a great deal of patience and persistence. And I have to admit, I was embarrassed more than once. Some people might call that failure. But with each time that I wasn't at my best, I was actually taking a step toward getting better. It was a form of training, if you will. The fact is, I was the only one who could control the outcome. If I had listened to people who told me I couldn't do it or shouldn't do it, I wouldn't be sitting here talking to you today."

"Maybe you got lucky, John. I might not be as lucky," Heidi said.

"Was it luck? Was it coincidence? No, it wasn't either of those things. It wasn't even talent. It was doing the work and sticking with it for the long run."

"What do you do if something goes wrong? Automatically, we all do the same thing. We ask ourselves: Who is to blame? Why does this crap always happen to me? We quarrel with fate, look for culprits, and blame others. It's a natural tendency. But let me ask you once again, Heidi, who is sitting in the driver's seat of your life now? Are you the pilot or the passenger?"

"I know I should be the pilot, but I feel like the passenger," Heidi said.

"Well, if you sit in the back, you don't get to decide where you arrive. If I had looked for culprits, I would never have been so successful. But I didn't do that. I didn't stand up and say it had to be somebody's else's fault that I had to overcome things nobody else did. That didn't even occur to me," John said. "The only thing I wanted to know was how I could do better. What could I do differently to get different results?"

"Okay, so I need to ask myself what I can do differently to get different results, right?" Heidi asked.

"That's right. Stop bemoaning about what other people won't do and start figuring out what *you* can do. You see, it's never the circumstances that decide our success or failure—it's how we respond to those circumstances. My advice to you is that you should never give that type of control to other people. Stay in the pilot's seat, where you have control. Control your focus; otherwise, you will be controlled. Don't blame the bank or your bank account. Turn your focus on what you can do right now. Take the wheel, Heidi," he said. "This is a setback, but it's not a game ender. Don't let it kill your dream—instead, use it to fuel your dream and motivate you to find a way to get past this wham!, as well as any others that will come your way."

"I guess I can explore other options. Maybe I can get the nerve up to ask my folks for a loan or see if they're interested in investing in my business ..." Heidi mused.

"That's a possibility. Or maybe you can take the controls and do something different," John suggested.

"Like what? Do you have any ideas?" she asked.

"Maybe, Heidi, you can find someone who has a food truck or stand who will let you rent it on the weekends or once or twice a month. It will give you some experience, and it might help you get that business experience that you need to get a loan. It's a big city—I think if you're creative, you'll find a way to make it happen. Just don't hand the controls to someone else, because they'll veer you off course every time. They might even keep your dreams from taking flight," John said.

"But now, let's turn to your job here—I heard there is talk of a reorganization in the next few months. If that happens, I expect some changes around here, which might open up an opportunity that may interest you," he said.

They spent the remainder of the hour discussing the possible changes and Heidi's experience and qualifications. At first, Heidi wasn't certain any of the potential changes would provide her with a new opportunity in the company, but as John pointed out her strengths, he convinced her that her doubts were nothing more than a lack of confidence and her natural tendency to shy away from things that were outside of her realm of experience.

"Just because you haven't done this before, that doesn't mean you can't do it, Heidi. Many responsibilities are derived from talents and skills you do have; you just can't connect them," John said.

"I get that," Heidi answered. "But what if it's not my dream job, where I want to end up for the rest of my career?"

"It probably won't be!" John agreed. "It will most likely be a steppingstone, giving you the experience and leverage to climb up the ladder, where you will hopefully find your dream. I know—I've changed jobs 11 times, Heidi. Six of those were before I came to the company. And after I got here, I've held several different positions, each one with a bit more responsibility than the last. You will never start out where you want to end up, that's just not possible. However, if you're in the pilot's seat, you'll always know where you are and where you're going. So what do you say? Are you ready to jump behind the wheel and take your career here to the next level? Do you want to go for it?"

"Well, now that you put it that way, yes. Let's do it!"

Chapter Four

THE TWO P's:
POSITIVITY AND PRECISION

Heidi felt like she needed to take a step back and reassess the whole food truck thing. It wasn't that she was giving up, but she had to admit that it seemed overwhelming. She would need funding, equipment—which included the evasive truck—and that was just the start of it. After a bit of research, she learned that she would need a license to prepare and sell food. And it would be in her best interests to take a food handler training course and receive her certification. Common sense prevailed, and she determined that obtaining a food truck was premature—a bit like putting the cart before the horse. After all, she wouldn't need it until she was certified and licensed. So she adopted a new mantra—first things first. It would take time, but that was one thing she had an abundance of when she wasn't working.

While it seemed like she was putting her new idea on hold, she knew she was being responsible. Like John said, she was reinforcing her chances for success by becoming knowledgeable and learning the trade before she jumped in with both feet. She had even decided not to tell her family about her dream—she didn't think she could handle it if they were like her friend, Emily, and laughed at her.

Yes, John had reinforced the need for a positive mindset, but it was someone else who shared that she needed something just as important—something that hadn't occurred to her at all.

Heidi had only met her cousin, Mia, twice during her life, once when her family visited her grandmother's family in Germany, and once when Mia and her mother, Heidi's aunt, visited the States for a month when Heidi was a teenager. She and Mia didn't know each other very well, but Heidi looked up to her cousin, who was five years older than she was. When she heard Mia would be visiting their family, she found that she was excited to reconnect with her, this time as an adult. Their age difference wouldn't matter as much as it had when they were younger, and Heidi really looked forward to the visit.

Of course, her mother spent weeks preparing for the visit, which Heidi found amusing. Her mother often went overboard, wanting to impress. But Heidi reminded her that Mia was there to spend time with their family, not to inspect their house or accommodations.

Knowing that her mother would fret over her cousin, Heidi gladly volunteered to pick Mia up from the airport. It would give the two a chance to catch up and get to know each other again before Mia was bombarded by the whole family.

As soon as Mia appeared, Heidi recognized her right away. She still looked like the Mia she had admired as a child, but now Heidi saw an adult, instead of a teenager. She was dressed comfortably, but showed no sign that she'd just endured a long flight with a couple layovers. Heidi smiled as she watched Mia confidently and seemingly effortlessly carry her luggage toward her.

The two exchanged warm greetings.

"Look at you, Heidi! You're all grown up!" Mia exclaimed.

"It's been a while. I'm no longer the awkward little 13 year old who followed you around everywhere you went," Heidi laughed.

On the way home, they talked like they were old friends, catching up on each other's lives.

"So, Mia, my mom said you work for an engineering firm. That must be exciting," Heidi said.

"It can be. But it can also be very detailed work. As you can imagine, we have to be very precise in everything we do. But I like it. What about you, Heidi? What are you doing now that you're all grown up?" Mia asked.

"Well, when I graduated from college, I accepted a position in the marketing department at a mid-size firm. I like it, but it's not what I want to do forever," Heidi answered.

"Oh? What do you want to do?"

"Well, I'm not sure. As a child, you might remember, I always wanted to be a high-powered executive. A part of me still wants that to happen," Heidi said.

"And the other part? What does it want, Heidi?" Mia asked.

Heidi hesitated a moment, considering whether she should say anything. In the end, she decided she could trust Mia.

"Mia, I haven't shared this with my family yet, but lately, I've been entertaining the idea of opening a German eatery—but not a restaurant. I'm toying with the concept of operating a food truck. There would be less work, shorter hours, and a lot less overhead," Heidi replied.

"Really? A food truck? That's interesting! I didn't know German food was big in the States."

"From what I've seen, Mia, Americans love different cuisines, especially when they are new and different. There are a handful of German restaurants around here, but the food isn't really authentic—you know, like our grandmother's. I want to bring authentic German food to the people, and a food truck will enable me to bring it to them in their neighborhood," Heidi said.

"So what's stopping you?" Mia asked her cousin.

"A few things—there are a lot of logistics to work out, like how I'm going to fund the investment and the fact that I have a lot to learn. I have to get certified in food safety and sanitation and learn what it takes to be an entrepreneur. And I've decided I'm going to keep my full-time job, at least for a while … if I even decide to move forward and do this."

"Okay, tell me again, what's stopping you?" Mia asked.

"I guess I'm not sure it's a good idea. Going into business can be risky, and there's always a chance that I'll fail. My friend, Emily, seems to think there's a big chance of that," Heidi sighed.

"She's your friend, and she's doomed you to failure before you even start?" Mia asked with surprise in her voice.

"I know how it sounds, but she means well. She's just trying to protect me," Heidi said.

"Hmmm, well, if there's one thing I know it's that if you want to succeed, you have to have a positive mindset. You have to believe in yourself, wholeheartedly. Because if you don't, you'll give up at the first sign of trouble," Mia remarked.

"That's what John, my mentor, has been saying. But I'm a realist, Mia, and I realize that there's always a chance …"

Mia interrupted before Heidi could finish.

"Heidi, can I stop you right here for a second? First, you *do* need a positive mindset—you need to be your own best advocate. You have to sell yourself on this idea before you can sell your idea to anyone else. But that's not all—you can have an unfaltering belief in your idea and your business, but even then, that's not enough," Mia said.

"There's more? What else do I need?" Heidi asked, somewhat exasperated.

"Heidi, we come from a German family. You know the stereotype? That Germans are strict and rigid, stubborn— things are just so? Well, that's what I deal with at work. Things have to be just so—there can be no room for error in engineering, for that would cause certain failure," said Mia.

"So, you're saying I have to be perfect and can't make any mistakes? Oh no, I am doomed," Heidi replied.

"No, we all fail. But we forget that there are tools that can help us be better. While we may not be perfect, per se, especially the first time, we can strive to be exceptional. My company doesn't expect perfection, but they do expect precision—attention to detail, even the little things. Have you ever heard the term 'German precision?'" Mia laughed.

"I sure have! You're saying it's a real thing?" Heidi answered.

"Precision is very real, and in my company, it is an expectation. Without it, there could be a failure, maybe even a catastrophe. Actually, if it was a principle adopted more frequently across the business world, even across the globe, we would see higher quality, improved efficiency, and far fewer failures," Mia advised.

"This is interesting, Mia. I think I can learn a lot from you. Do you mind teaching your younger cousin a thing or two while you're here? I'll be happy to keep you well fed with some authentic German food. It will be like you never left home," Heidi laughed.

"Heidi, I'd love to help you in any way I can. But you don't have to go out of your way to make me any German food. To tell you the truth, I was hoping I could enjoy some 'authentic' American fare while I'm here. Maybe some hamburgers, pizza, and tacos?" she laughed.

"Well, none of those are actually American," Heidi laughed, "but I guarantee there's no shortage of places to get your fill of them. Just don't tell Mom—I think she's been cooking since she heard you were coming!"

Chapter Five

TRAINING IS THE KEY TO SUCCESS

During the next two weeks, Heidi and Mia spent as much time together as possible. Heidi took Mia to see all the tourist sites, and they had fun shopping and enjoying their fair share of pizza and tacos. They found they had a lot in common—they liked the same toppings on their pizza and had similar tastes in clothing. Neither liked wearing hats, and both loved wearing heels. They even enjoyed listening to the same music.

But it wasn't all fun—the two had several serious discussions, as well. It was over lunch at an outdoor café that Mia brought up Heidi's dream again.

"So, Heidi, are you serious about it … or not? Because if you are, I want to help you," Mia offered.

"I don't know. Sometimes the idea is overwhelming. It would be great if I actually did succeed, Mia, but what if I don't? What if I fail?" Heidi asked.

"Oh, Heidi, you keep looking at everything that could go wrong. But maybe you need to look in a mirror," Mia suggested.

"Why?" Heidi asked.

"Because sometimes the worst adversary you can find in your quest for success is yourself. Right now, it seems to me that the you are the biggest thing standing in your own way," Mia pointed out.

"If only I had hindsight, that would help," Heidi admitted.

"Well, you don't. Nobody has that pleasure. But you do have something, and it's important," Mia said.

"What's that?"

"You have the ability to strengthen yourself. Heidi, success doesn't just come your way—it's a muscle that has to be trained. Train it," said Mia. "You say you're not doing what you really want to do at work. You want to be an executive. Train that muscle. If you haven't found success in that area yet, you've been training the wrong muscle. You've been training the excuse muscle—the 'it's not fair' muscle and the 'there aren't any opportunities for me' muscle. Heidi, I know I sound insensitive, but it's true. Where's the 'Heidi can do it' muscle? Is it in there?"

"I'm trying to find it, Mia. I've even found a mentor to help me. John is great, and he's pointed out a few things I've been working on," Heidi answered. "For example, he also said that success is a muscle. And I understand this, but there really haven't been opportunities for me to climb the corporate ladder, Mia."

"You might not want to hear this, Heidi, but I'm going to give you some tough love. Your biggest enemy is not the circumstances, the fate, other people or the competition. Your biggest enemy is your autopilot. It's what you do every day, without thinking about it or the fact that it impacts your success."

"What kind of things are you talking about?" Heidi asked.

"Often, it's not things you *are* doing, but things you *aren't* doing. Over 90% of the day, you don't think about what you are doing. You're just doing what you've always done. You've programmed yourself, your actions, your attitudes, and your routine. If you want to arrive somewhere else in the future than where you have been in the past, you have to reprogram yourself."

"Let me explain," Mia continued. "Heidi, I was taught this by a very good friend. For some reason, he took me under his wing and became a mentor of sorts to me. Because of him, I was able to train my success muscle. Once I knew how he changed his life around, I knew I could do it, too."

"What did he do?"

"His story is an interesting one, Heidi. He was young, in his mid-20s, and he was a success, by all appearances. He even owned a Porsche! But by the time he was 30, he was flat broke. He founded a start-up company, and at first, it all went great. But then he made a few wrong decisions and, above all, had the wrong people around him, people who gave him bad advice. As you probably know, a young company doesn't have a great deal of reserves. Within weeks, it got so bad that he lost everything—his car, his apartment, his friends, and even his pride. Naturally, he almost gave up. He blamed it on fate, he hated his clients, and he felt sorry for himself. Those things didn't help. Having a pity party did him no good. After all, he was still broke," Mia explained.

"Wow. So what did he do?" Heidi asked.

"He had to do some deep thinking. When he did, he realized that the only person he had to blame was himself. Nobody had forced him to make these decisions or trust those people. He did that on his own. And do you know why he did? It was because his autopilot was working toward failure, not success. He kept doing what he'd always done, even when it wasn't working. He had to totally retrain his success muscle, so it worked for him, not against him. He finally decided that it was time to start acting and performing like a winner, not a loser," Mia said.

"I don't get how that changed his results, though, Mia," Heidi admitted.

"You can't focus on what you don't want, Heidi. You see, he didn't want to fail. He didn't want to be a loser. So, that's what he focused on—what he didn't want! You cannot be successful when you focus on what you don't want, Heidi. It's impossible. It's like pushing success away every time it tries to get closer."

"And that is what I'm doing, isn't it, Mia? I'm focusing on what I don't want—I don't want to stay in my position for years. I don't want to take a risk because I might fail," Heidi realized.

"Precisely, Heidi. But to understand that, my friend had to fail. But you know what happened when he did? He lost everything. The worst thing that could happen actually did happen. When it did, he didn't have anything else to fear, so he accepted it and turned things around. This time, though, he focused on what made him happy. Success wasn't all about money anymore—it was about people and happiness. Once he realized that, he trained completely new muscles and reprogrammed his autopilot to bring him what he did want, not what he didn't want."

"Amazing. Mia, do you think that's my problem?" Heidi asked.

"Only you can answer that, Heidi. Do you take on something and don't do it? Do you find thousands of reasons why it's not a good time, why today is not the day? Are the same obstacles in front of you all the time, and you don't know why? If you can answer yes to any of those questions, then yes, I think that might be your problem," Mia said.

"Can you help me retrain my muscle so I can reprogram myself?" Heidi asked hopefully.

"I'm willing if you are!" Mia agreed. "It's like reprogramming yourself so you're on autopilot toward what you really do want, but this time, with German precision so you don't go off course. The first step is you have to reprogram yourself every time you have a new goal. You can't do what you did yesterday to get what you want today."

"I think I get it. I can't just sit here and hope that something is going to happen. I have to take steps toward what I want, or I'm going to keep getting the same results I've always gotten, which is what I don't want. Right?" Heidi asked.

"That's right! You have to create new habits for yourself and define new muscles for your success and train them. I think you've started doing this by getting a mentor and working with him. You're training your muscle, but you're not using it yet. That's okay—you want that muscle to be fully trained and ready to go when you're ready. I think you've got what it takes to succeed, Heidi, but it's up to you if you do anything with it," Mia said.

Chapter Six

HAVE THE COURAGE
TO BE OUTSTANDING

Just as John had predicted, a reorganization was underway, and it created several new openings. The position John had encouraged her to apply for was, in her opinion, a bit out of her league. However, John assured her that his experience with the company had taught him that they weren't always looking for someone with experience specific to the skills for that position. Most of the time, they were looking for an individual who showed promise and had leadership skills that would lend themselves well to that department or role. In other words, if she was doing a commendable job in her current position, the hiring committee would trust that she would be able to master different responsibilities, as long as she had the desired traits and characteristics they were looking for.

Admittedly, the position was not one she would have applied for without John's encouragement. Normally, she would have climbed the corporate ladder step by step, never straying from the hierarchy that had long been established at the company. But John reminded her that she was the pilot of her career, and she was in control of where it went. He also pointed out that this position could lead to further advancement because it would broaden her experience and skills.

But then he told her that could only happen if she stepped up and committed to being not just good, but outstanding. Starting at this moment, he urged her to put a higher level of expectation on herself in her current role, and as an applicant for a higher position within the organization.

"Heidi, there will be others applying for this position. Some will have experience in the department; some won't. I can tell you that all of them will have one thing in common—they will be qualified, based on the job description. I can also tell you one more thing—few, if any, of them will be outstanding. And that's where you come in," John said.

"John, I don't think I'm there quite yet. I have been training my success muscle and making changes in my daily routine and habits. But I'm still a work in progress. I'm not outstanding. I do my job, and I feel I do it very well, but if I was outstanding, I think I would have been sought out for a promotion before now," she replied.

"Heidi, you are normal in many ways. We are all expected to do our jobs and do them well. That's not a selling or promotional point. It's an expectation. What makes someone promotional, though, isn't that they do what's expected. Anyone can be normal. Who needs that? We need outstanding … and even though you don't see that as a requirement for the position, it most certainly is a strong one."

"Let me put it this way, Heidi. Let's say you have that food truck, and you're out there selling your cuisine to customers around town. But then suddenly you find that there are ten more food trucks that are now also serving German food … and they're all good. How is your business going to survive, or even thrive, with all that competition?" John asked.

"Umm, I have to be better than the rest. My food has to be better?" Heidi answered, hesitantly.

"That's right. You wouldn't have to worry about the competition if they were all good, but you were outstanding! Now, apply that to this opportunity. The other applicants might all be good, so your job is to figure out where you are outstanding."

"That's what I can't figure out, John. I'm not positive that I would be the best applicant. What if I go into the interview and fall short? What if they laugh at me for thinking I actually qualify? And then the next time a position opens up, they won't even consider me? If I'm not convinced that I'm outstanding enough to be the best applicant for this position, how will I ever convince the interview committee that I am?" Heidi asked.

"Heidi, when we first met, you told me that you felt you were ready for a promotion. You believed you had what it takes to move up the ladder and were frustrated because that wasn't happening. In short, you had confidence in yourself then, but now you are second guessing yourself. I think it's time for me to share a lesson I learned years ago with you," he said.

"Go ahead. I'd love to hear it," Heidi replied.

"Okay, here goes. I already told you about my stuttering. I know this might be hard to believe, but I was once also shy, insecure, and afraid of strangers. When I talked to people I didn't know well, my face would turn red and I stuttered. Of course, other people could see this. Anytime I had to speak to a stranger or a group of people I didn't know, I got stage fright. Yet, Heidi, today, I speak at our national sales meetings in front of thousands of people, and I do it without any fear or anxiety. And I don't have to overcome myself or my doubts. In fact, I think it's awesome! I actually love every minute of it. But that wasn't something that came naturally to me. I had to learn it. I had to overcome my doubts, fears, and anxiety and become confident. I have learned to use my potential. That wouldn't have happened if I'd said, 'Oh, no way, I can't do that. I can't call or talk to a bunch of strangers.' I've learned to try it before I say I can't. And that takes courage," John shared."

"John, no one would ever know now that you once were uncomfortable speaking in front of people. As a matter of fact, you are considered to be a gifted speaker. I know quite a few people who have enjoyed listening to you and who comment on your eloquent delivery," Heidi remarked.

"Thank you. But it could have gone the other way if I had let my lack of confidence stand in the way. Realistically, though, I was my own worst enemy. Speaking, like so many things, isn't something that everyone does extremely well the first time. But it was something I could have never done extremely well if I hadn't done it the first time," he pointed out.

"Heidi, I believe you are ready for this position … sure, you might need training in some the areas specific to that department, but you have everything else you need. But before we get to that, we have to get you out of your own way and get you to start thinking that you *can*, instead of *can't*. It's a common obstacle, actually. It's a pitfall that we all fall into at some time. How many times do we think I can't? I am not good enough. I still need time. I don't dare try and risk disappointment, or worse, embarrassment. Sound familiar?"

Smiling, Heidi nodded. "It sure does, John. I've been reprogramming myself so I think in terms of success about owning a food truck. But in the corporate arena, I haven't had a lot of positive reinforcement."

"Well, I'm here to tell you that you can do it. You just don't know it yet."

"How can I ever know it?" Heidi asked.

"You have to try. Success doesn't work without courage. Success doesn't work without trying. You'll never know what you really can do if you don't try. And to convince you, I want you to ask yourself the right questions," he said. "Get out your notepad, because I want you to write them down."

Heidi quickly grabbed her pen and opened her notebook. She jotted down the questions as John rattled them off:

- What happens if I never try? What will I lose; what becomes impossible?
- What do I achieve if I try? It's not what can go wrong, but about chances, value, and possible benefits.
- Now, ask yourself the signature question: What would I do if I had no fear?

"Try it, Heidi. Answer those questions as honestly as you can. Then, to convince yourself beyond a shadow of a doubt, I want you to repeat those questions—not once, not 10 times, not 50,000 times—but 70 times. Tell yourself why you are capable and why you are worthy and why you *can* achieve success 70 times, and believe me, you will believe it. Don't be your own worst enemy. Start telling yourself what is possible, instead of what is not possible. It will change your life."

"That's different, and it takes a self-assessment—an honest look at where you excel. What are your strengths? What do you do better than most? Everyone is outstanding in some way; most are outstanding in multiple ways. Let's identify your outstanding traits and your achievements first, and then I will show you how they can relate to the desired qualifications for this position," John said.

"Okay, I can do that. But what happens if I don't get the job and this is all just a waste of time?" Heidi asked.

"Then you lost a few hours of your time, that's all. But you still have your new mindset. What's the worst that can happen? You don't get the job, but you still have your current position. You can still learn and grow. You can become more experienced. You can get a no, but keep on plugging away until you get a yes, then another, and another. You have nothing to lose if you try. At the very least, you will gain some valuable experience. But you never know what you might have lost if you don't try."

"You're right. This is what I wanted. It's one of my dreams, being an executive and helping others. I just thought I was ready. I guess I'm not so ready, after all. It looks like I still have some work to do," Heidi said, almost thinking out loud.

"Yes, you have work to do, but remember, you already have everything you need. You can be trained to do anything you don't know how to do. But that's not what anyone looks for in a leader. They're looking for someone with those qualifications and skills that can't be taught," John advised.

"Do you mind sharing what those are?" Heidi inquired.

"Well, we covered two of them here today—courage and confidence. Work on those questions and your answers, and I think you'll find that you have what it takes. Then go over them again and again, until you're not only good at answering them, but you're outstanding at it. That's what will make you stand out from the rest."

"It's kind of like practice until perfect, isn't it, John?" Heidi asked.

"Yes, just like that. You'll get better and better each time. Before you know it, you'll be so good that everyone will think you were born to be a leader—most of all, you will be one of them. And, hey, if it doesn't work, figure out why, or give it up and try something new. Anything is possible when you have the courage and the confidence to give it a try."

Chapter Seven

EVERYTHING IS POSSIBLE

Following the announcement of a reorganization came the news that the company would be manufacturing and marketing a new product. The announcement created uncertainty and fear among some in her department—change always had that tendency. Internal reorganizations typically meant changes in leaderships, transfers between departments, or potential changes in employees' roles. And there was always the underlying, but often unspoken fear, that a major reorganization or the addition of a new product or new direction could close a department or division entirely, resulting in job losses.

Heidi was fortunate because John had some insight into the reorganization and had assured her that this change entailed growth, not cutbacks. It was precisely for that reason that he encouraged her to apply and prepare for a managerial position within the new department.

Heidi focused on the preparation—she did the Q and A John had given her, not once, not twice, but dozens of times until her answers weren't just memorized, but truly ingrained into her belief system. In the process, she found herself becoming excited about the potential career change and the impact it would have on not only her pocketbook, but her future.

In the meantime, John coached her through the interview process and her responses to probable questions. What were her strengths and weaknesses? What was her greatest accomplishment? What difficulties had she overcome? And where did she see herself in five and ten years? These were all questions that were likely to be posed in order to ascertain Heidi's leadership ability and determine if she had the vision and experience to grow within the organization.

In the process, Heidi learned a lot about herself and her leadership style. She discovered she was a collaborator who enjoyed working closely with others. John assured her that this was a good trait, one that would lend itself well in a new department, where everyone would be new to their role and, therefore, learning together. He also pointed out that it would contribute to her success as an entrepreneur one day, if she still wanted to pursue that path.

However, now that a potential promotion was a possibility, Heidi found that her desire to be a business executive was renewed ... and her desire to open her own business diminished. Rather than being disillusioned and frustrated, she found that she was excited and energized. It was like all of her childhood dreams were within reach, and she knew if she didn't pursue them, she would regret not knowing what could have been.

To her excitement, she made it through the first round of interviews, and John was more than willing to help her prepare for her next, likely more intense, interview.

"Your management style and goals are going to be investigated in the next interview, Heidi, so we need to delve into those in preparation. These are areas that you need to be confident about, so you need to be able to identify and support your goals when asked," he said.

Heidi knew her goals—she'd known what they were since she was a child. She wanted to implement her business style and policies to grow a company and its employees. She wanted the flexibility to make decisions that could potentially make transformational changes that would benefit an organization and those they served. This position was a steppingstone that would get her closer to her childhood dream, and she was prepared to do whatever it took to improve her chances of getting the promotion.

That is precisely what she told Mia when they talked over the weekend.

"I'm so excited! Finally, my career is showing promise!" Heidi exclaimed.

"It sure looks like it is, Heidi. I'm very happy for you. But if I can ask, what about your dream of owning your own business? Remember the food truck and how excited you were about that?" her cousin asked.

"Yes, and that's still a thought, but right now, things are turning around at work. For the first time, I see a real opportunity—one that is within my reach. I need to go for it, Mia. If I don't, I might always regret it. And if there's one thing John has taught me, it's that I need to be persistent— to follow through and not give up. Things won't happen overnight, but if I apply myself and keep improving, they will happen!"

"Well, I agree with John. We are all a work in progress, and it looks like you're making real progress right now. I'm happy for you, Heidi. And I know you have what it takes to succeed. Just don't lose sight of the details when you're striving for the bigger long-term goal. It's the day to day that creates the type of precision and perfection for success," Mia said. "Letting the little things slide can cause big problems. But as I learned in engineering, when you focus on minor details, as well as the long-term picture, everything and anything is possible."

Mia's support meant the world to Heidi, but it was ultimately John who gave her the insight that helped her see herself as a candidate for the job from the perspective of those who really mattered—the interview committee.

It was their last meeting before her scheduled interview, and Heidi shared Mia's encouraging words with her mentor. Once again, John responded with a life lesson that made a lasting impression on her.

"Heidi, you have to get there first. It doesn't matter if you are planning the coolest trip, designing a prototype, pursuing the best dream, or if you have the best idea and the most extensive training. None of that will do you any good if nobody knows you exist," he advised.

"Now, I don't want you to be confused by that. Of course, they know you exist—they are interviewing you, after all. But don't forget, they aren't hiring what you have to sell—they're hiring you. Ideas will always fluctuate and change, but the person behind those ideas will remain the same. What I'm trying to say is you have to sell yourself. If you don't sell yourself at your best, who will do it?"

"I'm not sure I understand exactly what you're trying to say, John," Heidi said.

"Often, we have a hard time selling ourselves. We think we are not sellers. That is nonsense. We all come into the world as salesmen. In fact, children are the best salesmen, we just let life take us back down again—you know, we become modest, listen to negativity and criticism, and eventually forget how to sell ourselves to the world. It's sad, actually. And we have to bring this ability back to us. If we don't, the competition will always pass us up."

"I know you're educated and knowledgeable, Heidi. You've proven that. However, knowledge alone is no longer enough. Academic degrees are no longer enough. We live in a time where we are flooded with knowledge, academics, and information. But it's not the person who has all of that knowledge and information who gets noticed and stands out. It's the individual who manages to become visible in the data jungle and manages to market himself. Like your cousin, Mia, says, everything is possible—but I will add that everything is possible to those who figure out how to market themselves the best."

"Oh no! John, have I been focusing on the wrong things?"

"No, everything we've worked on thus far will contribute to your ultimate success. However, I want to shift you away from focusing on your USP so you can work on your UPP," John said.

"My UPP? Now I'm really confused," Heidi said.

"Your USP is your unique selling proposition. However, in my opinion, the USP is dead. The only thing that makes you unique is your personality, your individual abilities, and your talents, values, and beliefs. So instead of focusing on your USP, you need to focus on your UPP— your unique personal proposition."

"Hmmm, interesting. Tell me more ..."

"Heidi, if you want this job—or any job, for that matter—the most important factors are no longer what you can do or what you know. Today, who you are is far more important. Why should they hire *you?* In a nutshell, what used to be the product is now the relationship. What used to be information is now emotion—yes, emotion does impact business decisions. And what used to be knowledge is now personality."

"So when you walk into that interview, don't sell your experience or your resume. Don't sell your education or your seniority. Sell yourself. If you can do that, people will notice you and you will stand out. If you do that, Heidi, then everything really is possible."

Chapter Eight

RELATIONSHIP MANAGEMENT

Barely able to contain her excitement, Heidi exclaimed, "I got the promotion!" when she walked through John's office doorway.

"Congratulations, Heidi! I'm very proud of you and happy for you," he replied with sincerity.

"I couldn't have done it without you, John. I owe it all to you."

"You did this on your own—you reached your first major milestone, and it's definitely something to celebrate," John remarked.

"I agree. John, I'm so excited to get started. I really want to make my mark and make a difference!"

"You will, and I'm sure of that. But realize that with each change comes new and different challenges. That's what growth is about," he pointed out.

"I look forward to them! I'm ready, really ready for this role and any challenges that come my way," Heidi assured him. "I've got so much to do. After all, I have a brand new department to get up and running, and employees to train, and …"

"Yes, you do," John smiled. "It can be overwhelming. But I'll be here to help you—that won't change."

"Thanks, John. I appreciate that very much. But for now, I think I need to focus most of my time and attention on my responsibilities. So, maybe it would be best if we didn't meet as often—if that's okay with you?" she asked.

"If that's what you prefer, Heidi, I respect your wishes. But if you need me, and I think you will, you know where to find me. Just do yourself a favor, and don't let pride get in the way and try to do it all on your own for too long," he replied.

"I won't! But I think I have the confidence and tools I need to fly the plane without a co-pilot now! I need to spread my wings and see if I can do it."

"Keep in touch then, Heidi, and let me know how it's going," John said.

"Absolutely! And thanks again, John!"

* * *

Heidi's friend, Emily, shared in her excitement.

"See, I told you to stick with it. It's always been your dream to be a hot shot manager—and you did it! And you almost bought a food truck!" she laughed.

"Well, I had to go after the opportunity. And the food truck wasn't such a bad idea, Em. I just chose not to pursue it."

Mia also joined in with the congratulations, telling her that she always knew she was capable and was proud of her for her achievement. But then she followed with another question, "The world is at your feet! So what's next?"

Heidi simply laughed. She'd just been given a promotion. What was next was too far in the horizon to think about so soon.

Time told her that was the truth. Besides, she was so busy every day that she didn't have time to think about the future.

And her work was paying off. She built a team of skilled and talented people, and she gave them the support they needed to do their jobs and do them well. And as a member of the management team, she was building relationships with other supervisors and team leaders on a daily basis.

In the process, she never lost sight of John's advice and really strived to focus on relationships and remembering that, despite deadlines and demands, she needed to remember her unique personal proposition. Heidi found that it was a great tool for collaboration and cooperation—people wanted to contribute to the success of the team if they felt like they were appreciated.

It was about six months into her position, though, that she first became aware of a potential problem. Actually, she had noticed subtle signs of contention before, but they were now more pronounced and couldn't be ignored.

There was a weekly meeting of all department managers, during which time, progress and obstacles were discussed and expectations and deadlines were shared. During these meetings, Heidi noticed that one of the department supervisors often contradicted her suggestions and sometimes even pushed them aside without any consideration.

It had happened a time or two, and at first, Heidi thought it was her imagination. However, over time, it had become more obvious ... and uncomfortable—to the point that Heidi dreaded the weekly meetings altogether.

Knowing she was relatively new to her position, and the other manager had several years more experience, she was at a loss in how to approach the situation. It was then that she thought of John—he had told her to contact him if she needed him. Besides, he'd never steered her wrong in the past.

Thankfully, John readily agreed to meet with her.

"John, I have a unique situation, and I'm not sure how to handle it. At first, I didn't think it was a big deal, but it seems to be getting worse. I didn't want to bother you, but I wasn't sure what else I could do," she said.

After explaining the situation, John reminded her that this was one of those new challenges that he'd warned her about. While she had been prepared for him to side with her and tell her how to approach the situation, she wasn't prepared for John's actual response.

"Heidi, have you considered that the problem could be you?" he asked.

"Me? How? I haven't done anything to merit his disapproval, but it seems that is what I'm getting. How could this be my fault?" she asked.

"Let me ask, Heidi, have you had this problem with anyone else? Have you noticed any issues with any of your employees or any other members in the management team?"

"Um, no. My employees are good, and there haven't been any other issues. It just seems that no matter what I say, this guy contradicts it," she answered.

"Maybe the problem isn't in what you're saying. Maybe it's not in the facts or the suggestions. Maybe the problem is in the relationship. Have you considered that?" John asked.

"But why? What did I do to him to warrant this response?" Heidi asked, frustrated.

"Maybe it isn't what you did, but it might be what you didn't do. Every relationship is important … and that little tip applies even more the higher up the management chain you go. Can I ask what you've done to establish a relationship with him, if anything?"

Thinking for a moment, Heidi admitted that she hadn't done anything—negative or positive.

"Every personality is different. But I can tell you that every relationship is your responsibility—it is up to you to find out where the relationship falls short, and then how you can build it and make it stronger."

At the end of an hour, Heidi had learned that there was a possibility that her ideas and suggestions were being met with skepticism and criticism because she hadn't been vocal about lending support to the other managers. There was also the possibility that someone else might see the progress she was making as a threat or competition.

"So what do I do, John? How do I fix it?" Heidi asked.

"Seek him out. Ask for his suggestions. Ask how he would approach a situation. You cannot build or repair a relationship you haven't even established. Let him know you value him and his opinion. You might be surprised to find that when you do, he starts to value yours."

"That's great advice, John! I'm going to give it a try. I've been beside myself trying to figure out what I did wrong — and all this time, it could be as easy as what I didn't do."

"It's about relationship management, Heidi. You might have gotten the promotion, but you can't ever stop selling yourself," advised John.

"I won't forget that again. But, John, there's something else I stopped doing that I think I do need to start doing again," she said.

"What's that?" John asked.

"Meeting with you. I think I got a little overconfident and thought I knew it all — I'm embarrassed to admit that I believed I didn't need a mentor anymore. That was a mistake. I know now that I have more to learn. Is it okay if we return to our regular schedule, at least for a few months?" she asked, meekly.

"Absolutely — I look forward to it. Let's get started next Monday," John agreed.

"Perfect! I'll see you then," Heidi said.

"Oh, Heidi, before you leave, can I ask a favor?"

"Sure, what do you need?" she asked.

"I'd like your Monday special — some of those fabulous potato dumplings that I've grown to love," he smiled.

Laughing, Heidi agreed. "You got it, John. I'll bring a big helping!"

Chapter Nine

THE MOTHER OF ALL PSYCHOLOGY: QUESTIONS

John's advice worked, and Heidi made an effort to reach out to the other supervisors and managers in their division, and it was making a noticeable difference. However, as time went on and the department she oversaw established a workflow and had systems in place, new problems presented themselves.

As often happens, it appeared the honeymoon was over. Her department wasn't so new anymore, and with many of the initial challenges out of the way, they were getting pressure from upper management to improve their processes and increase production.

Heidi found herself in the middle, having to communicate and reinforce expectations to her team, while being frustrated with those same expectations. Sure, she understood what was being asked of her department and why ... but she wasn't given any input into those demands. Her opinion wasn't requested, and it seemed that she was simply the middleman who was responsible for carrying out someone else's orders. As a result, she felt like she didn't have a voice. It wasn't anything like the independent, rewarding, go-getter role she envisioned in her youth.

The truth be told, Heidi felt pressure, but her role wasn't giving her much satisfaction. She was carrying out someone else's ideas and policies to create success, but it really didn't feel like the success belonged to her. She worked long hours, attended more than a fair share of meetings, and walked away every day feeling like she had accomplished very little.

She'd been in her position for more than a year, and rather than feeling empowered, she felt discouraged. The satisfaction she'd always imagined just wasn't there.

Not wanting to admit defeat, Heidi kept her dissatisfaction to herself for a few months, but finally decided to tell John.

"It's not what I thought it would be, John. I feel like I'm constantly putting fires out and scrambling to keep up with new initiatives. I never have control or the freedom to put my management style and stamp on my department, let alone the company. I thought this was what I'd always wanted. What's wrong with me?" Heidi asked with a great deal of frustration.

"There is nothing wrong with you, Heidi. Sometimes, when we get what we want, we find out it wasn't what we wanted, after all. Sometimes, we discover that there are aspects of a career that don't suit our personality. And sometimes, there is something missing that would make all the difference, we just don't know what it is."

"I don't know what I'm supposed to do. I feel stagnant and stuck. Should I give it more time? Should I ask for different responsibilities, or more responsibility? It's all a guessing game, and if I don't understand why I'm not being fulfilled, I have no idea what I should do."

"Those are questions that only you can answer, Heidi. Maybe you're just experiencing a period of burnout, and it will pass. Maybe you need a different incentive and more inspiration. Only you can answer the questions weighing on your mind, and I know it's not an easy task. Asking yourself hard questions is the mother of all psychology. I can't tell you what questions to ask or what those answers will be. But I can give you some tools that can help," John offered.

"Please do. I don't know where else to turn, John," Heidi admitted.

"For starters, I can tell you that, while this seems to be a logical issue, it is not. On the contrary, it is emotional. If you want to know what to do, the best thing you can do is follow your heart. Your mind, your head, has a way of steering you wrong. It gets logical and argumentative. It tries to reason with you. Your heart, on the other hand, will rarely let you down."

"That makes sense. But how do I know what's in my heart?" she asked.

John reached into his desk drawer and pulled out a black spiral-bound notebook.

"Do you know what this is, Heidi?" he asked.

"Of course. It's a notebook, but what is it for?"

"It's my wish book," he smiled. "I've had this particular book for ten years. It's actually my second wish book, Heidi."

"What exactly is a wish book?" she asked.

"For the past 20 years, I've kept this book or one like it. It's a log of my daily wishes. Think of it as journal of sorts, documenting the things I want over time. Sometimes I wish for a new car or a promotion. Sometimes I wish for happiness or less stress. It doesn't matter what I wish for — it could be anything — but I always write it down."

"Why?"

"It reminds me of what is important to me. You see, not only do I write down what I wish for, but I review my wishes on a regular basis. And when I do, I discover things about myself. I learn what really matters to me, and what I really want .... without the day-to-day demands or pressures. In my reviews, I can sometimes see recurring wishes, which tells me these are not just trending or passing wishes, but something deeper and stronger. Sometimes, I can also see a common theme underlying my wishes—that's important for me to notice, as well. Sometimes, Heidi, I've even discovered that things I really thought I wanted weren't things I wanted at all. Sometimes, it was the opposite."

"Hmmm. That's interesting. So are you saying you want me to start a wish book, too?" she asked.

"I highly encourage it. Heidi, the answers you're seeking will require a great deal of self-discovery. You'll need to get to know yourself once again—on a deep level. That's how you'll gain an understanding of what's in your heart and where your heart is leading you."

On her way home from work that day, Heidi stopped at the local office supply store and bought herself a spiral-bound notebook. With a marker, she wrote "WISH BOOK" in capital letters across the front … and then she sat and looked at it, not knowing what to write. After spending her life always wishing for something, she was surprised that her mind was blank.

Thinking a walk would clear her head, she grabbed her jacket and went out the door. Her apartment was just a few blocks away from several markets and shops—maybe a little window shopping and a bite to eat would provide her with some inspiration.

It didn't take long before she was caught up in the sights, sounds, and smells. The outdoor cafes were in full swing, and vendors were selling their wares in pop-up shops. People walked the streets, pausing to admire vintage goods, jewelry, and tech gadgets, while carrying a cup of coffee, ice cream cone, or an oversized walking taco.

Heidi's mind quickly turned to her shelved dream of opening a food truck. She smiled to herself, imagining being a part of this environment and catering to the men, women, and children who were the pulse of this thriving community. It was an area that she'd been proud to show her cousin, Mia, when she had visited, and Heidi found it had been too long since she'd taken the time to enjoy the atmosphere.

Looking up, she noticed a business on the corner that hadn't been there before. The lack of a sign over the door piqued her curiosity. Intrigued, she walked through the entrance and found herself in a room with dogs and cats, and a couple parents with a handful of children who watched them with delight.

"Hi, can I help you?"

She was greeted by a male who was holding a leash in each hand.

"Um, no. There wasn't a sign on the door, so I decided to come in and see what type of business set up shop here. I didn't expect a pet store," Heidi said with smile.

"Actually, we are a rescue. This is one of the adoption events we hold throughout the community. The business is empty at the moment, but the owner has been generous and allowed us to use this space a couple times a week to introduce the pets to the public," the man said.

"Sounds like a good deal," Heidi replied.

"Hey, are you interested in meeting our animals? We have a lot of kittens, a few puppies, and a couple senior dogs that would make fantastic companions."

"Who, me? Oh, no, thanks—I like animals, but I don't think so. Not right now, anyway," Heidi answered.

"Well, why don't you walk around and meet one or two? Who knows, you might just fall in love! If you have any questions, just yell. My name is Chad, by the way."

"Thanks, Chad. I don't think I'm going to change my mind. I'm just window shopping today," she laughed.

"Go ahead, shop away—if you change your mind, just let me know!" he laughed.

Heidi slowly walked through the shop, smiling at the cute little puppies that were unable to contain their excitement at the prospect of being held or petted. Chad was right—they were so adorable that it would be easy to fall in love with any of them. But it was when she went to the back of the store that the animals really tugged at her heart. There were three larger, obviously older dogs, whose eyes spoke of sadness, even resignation.

"Sad, isn't it?"

Heidi turned to find Chad standing behind her.

"Yes. Doesn't anyone want them?" Heidi asked.

"Seniors are more difficult to place. Most people want a puppy. But older dogs are usually fully vetted and trained. We know their behaviors, and they require far less hands-on attention and care than more energetic younger dogs. Unfortunately for these guys, they know what it's like to be in a loving home … and they don't understand what happened," Chad explained.

"They look like they're lonely—almost like they're grieving. How did they end up in a shelter, if I can ask?"

"The two over there are brother and sister. Their owner had medical issues and had to give them up when he moved into assisted living," he said, pointing at a couple buff and white mixed breed dogs sharing a kennel. "They'd be lost without each other, so we'd like them to be adopted and stay together. And that little girl over there is a schnauzer. She's about eight years old. She was brought to us by someone who found her wandering the streets. We tried to find her owner but haven't had any luck. It's a shame, really, because she's a good dog. She would do best in a house without other pets, though. She's not keen about sharing attention."

"What's her name?" Heidi asked, bending down to pet her.

"I call her Jazz."

"That's an odd name, cute, but odd," she smiled.

"Well, she seems to like music. There was a festival not too long ago and a band was playing, and when she heard it, she just came to life," Chad explained. "It really stuck in my mind. I've never seen a dog react to music that way."

"Have you volunteered here very long?" Heidi asked.

"You could say that. I founded the not-for-profit and run this rescue. I do a little bit of everything around here," he answered.

"I'm sorry—I shouldn't have assumed you were a volunteer. It sounds like a rewarding career, though—you must really love animals," Heidi remarked.

"I do. And don't worry—I take no offense—volunteers are held in high esteem here. Are you interested?"

"In volunteering? I'd have to think about that. There's just not much time after work and ..."

"It's okay. I get it. We're all busy. But if you change your mind, give me a call," he said, reaching into his pocket to hand her a business card. "We really could use the help."

"Thanks, I'll do that," she said. Then she reached down to pet the dog one more time. "Bye, Jazz. Maybe I'll see you again."

Turning, she thanked Chad for taking the time to talk to her and introduce her to the dogs.

"I promise, I will think about volunteering. You're doing a good thing here," she said.

"Thank you. But how will I know it's you, if you do call, that is?" he asked.

"My name is Heidi. There aren't too many people by that name anymore, so I doubt you'll confuse me with someone else," she said.

"I like the name. It's nice to meet you, Heidi. I hope to see you around. Come back anytime," Chad said before turning to greet a couple who had walked through the door.

Walking home, Heidi reflected on the visit. Chad seemed to know what he wanted to do with his life. She wished she could say the same, she thought, as she passed other vendors. Then, passing a row of food trucks, she realized she hadn't eaten and stopped to grab a walking taco to eat on the return trip. *I really wish I could get some schnitzel and a fried potato pancake,* she thought.

Suddenly, she realized that she'd come up with two wishes within moments of each other … and they both led her to a familiar place.

But was she ready? Was it what she really wanted?

Those were tough questions, and they left her feeling as uncertain and lost as the animals at the rescue looked. In a way, she was scared to ask, and answer, those questions.

Then, she asked herself the toughest question of all, "What would I do if I wasn't afraid?"

Chapter Ten

IF YOU WOULD HAVE KNOWN THE WAY, YOU WOULD HAVE TAKEN IT

She enjoyed the walk so much that she made it part of her routine. A couple times a week, she'd venture out and check out the goods, the food, and the sights and sounds of the community. Every time, she noticed something different or something new—and she relished the exploration.

And although she was tempted, she avoided going back to the rescue. She simply wasn't ready to make a commitment, either to volunteering or adopting. She voiced her reluctance to Mia when they talked.

"I'm just as lost as those animals who no longer have a home. I have no idea what I want to do with my life."

"You're doing well at work, right? I mean, you've been successful since your promotion, haven't you? So you don't want to see where that will take you?" Mia asked.

"I've had success. I've also had setbacks, but that's to be expected, I guess. Mia, the thing is, the success isn't as satisfying as I thought it would be. What if it never is? What if I keep on climbing the proverbial ladder and find when I get to the top that I didn't want to be there, either? And let's not forget the possibility that I might never get there! I could spend my entire career unhappy, in a job that'll never take me to the place where I might be happy," Heidi sighed.

"What would make you happy, Heidi?"

"That's the million-dollar question, and I wish I knew. I've been keeping a wish book—it was John's idea. I write down the things I find myself wanting or wishing for, and, hopefully, that will lead me to what my heart really wants," Heidi explained.

"And what have those wishes been?" Mia asked. She had a knack for asking probing questions that cut right to the chase.

"Well, you won't believe this, but I actually had to stop myself because I found myself wishing I had a dog!" Heidi said, trying to avoid giving Mia the answers she was really looking for.

"A dog? How'd that come about?"

Heidi explained how she had met Chad and Jazz at the rescue's adoption event. "She really was a sweet dog, Mia. I just don't think it's the right time."

"Timing seems to be an issue with you. It's not the right time to volunteer. It's not the right time to adopt an orphaned dog. It's not the right time to make a change in your career. I think you've found yourself a universal excuse, Heidi. It's like you don't have to take any risks if you can keep putting your life on hold. Please don't get me wrong—it's just an observation, and I say it with love," Mia added.

"You might be right. I just wish I knew the right thing to do, the right path to take," Heidi admitted.

"Don't we all!" Mia exclaimed. "Wouldn't it be great if we all had hindsight or could predict the future? But we aren't given that luxury. Sometimes we have to take chances."

"Mia, if there is anything that is calling at me, it's still my desire to open a food truck. I've been bouncing the idea around in my head again, and I've thought of different things I could do to get started," Heidi said.

"Like what?"

"Well, I could start out part-time, catering special events. Or I could gauge interest and get my feet wet with a pop-up store—of course, that would limit the menu to just a few items, but it would be a start," Heidi said.

"Those sound like great ideas! Again, Heidi, what's stopping you?"

"I'm scared I'll be making a mistake, leaving behind a sure thing—a steady paycheck, benefits, and job security. What if I take a risk and find out I was wrong? My friend, Emily, seems to think it would be the wrong thing to do, and I cannot ignore the fact that she might be right."

"Nothing is certain, Heidi. I'm an engineer, and even when every detail is precise and it looks perfect on paper, there are still things that can go wrong. That can happen no matter what you do," Mia said. "Now, insofar as Emily, I will tell you that there is no right or wrong. Actually, the only thing wrong is the concept that something must be right or it is wrong! That's just untrue. You see, we often tend to judge if something is right or wrong. This is especially true when it comes to communication and relationships, just like you're seeing with Emily and her opinion. Emily tells you it's a mistake, and she wants to be the one who is right. And you're letting her win the debate," Mia pointed out.

"Heidi, at this point, the discussion about who is right is not helpful at all. It only leads deeper into the conflict. Instead of wallowing in the wrong or right question, it makes sense to look for a solution—and that solution is always in the future—the place of the great unknown."

"That's the hard part—not knowing," Heidi sighed again.

"What's right for Emily can't be right for you. Heidi, everybody has their own reality. My perception is different from yours, but perception is the basis or the individual concept we call reality. For that reason, what's right for me could be totally wrong for you! So forget right or wrong. That concept doesn't apply, and it shouldn't."

"You have a point, Mia. You always do. Between you and John, I know I have someone who will tell me like it is," Heidi said.

"We want what you want, Heidi. We want you to be happy. You've already tried the path you're on and it's not the ticket to your happiness, so what have you got to lose by trying a different path?"

"I'll think about it, Mia. I promise ..."

* * *

Heidi reiterated the conversation when she met with John two weeks later. As always, John listened patiently, letting her sort out her thoughts and feelings before offering any input.

"Heidi, when we first met, you didn't know where to turn. Do you remember that?"

"Of course I do, and you offered to mentor me ... because of you, I got a promotion. I couldn't have done it on my own!" Heidi exclaimed.

"Maybe you could have, but it's likely it would have taken longer. The point is, you didn't know which way to turn then, but that didn't stop you from taking advice from me, did it?" John asked.

"Not at all. It made me want your advice even more," Heidi countered.

"Heidi, if you knew the right way then, you would have taken it. But you didn't. You can't know if you're moving in the right direction if you're standing still. But sometimes that's where a mentor can help. You see, there are times when the answers are right in front of us, but we can't see them. That's when we need a mentor or someone to help us to discover our blind spot so we can get on track," he observed.

"Do I have a blind spot, John?" Heidi asked reluctantly.

"Yes, you do—we all do. You don't trust your heart. It's trying to tell you which way to go, but you aren't listening," he replied.

"It's just that I've invested so much in this career, John. My education, the years I've put in here, learning, and growing—and everything I learned from you. I don't want to throw all of that away," Heidi said with exasperation.

"You can take all of that with you—it's part of your growth. Everything you've learned is applicable in anything you do," he advised. "For now, though, you're standing still, and that will stifle your growth and motivation. You already reached a milestone here, but I think you're ready for a new, different milestone. I think you need a nudge, so I'm going to point in the direction you should take."

"What direction is that?" Heidi asked.

"I want you to find a way to get your feet wet. Cater a party or an event. Work with someone else who owns a food truck for a while. It's time for you to explore another direction—you can still turn around if it's not where you want to go, I assure you," he said.

"It's time? That's exciting … and scary. But I guess you're right. I would have been stuck in indecision forever if someone didn't give me a shove in the right direction," Heidi admitted.

"Don't be so hard on yourself, Heidi. Like I said, if you knew the right path to take, you would have taken it. Everyone needs a little nudge now and then. That's what I'm here for."

Chapter Eleven

HOW-TO: THE PLAN TO SUCCEED

With John's guidance, Heidi was ready to take the first step into entrepreneurship with renewed vigor. She walked through the neighborhood marketplace, checking out venues and exploring ideas. One day, on a whim, she walked into the pet rescue.

"Hi! You came back!" Chad greeted her as soon as she walked through the door.

"Yes, I thought I'd stop in and say hi and see how things are going," Heidi said.

"Are you ready to adopt?" he asked hopefully.

"Not just yet," she laughed. "But I wouldn't be averse to volunteering from time to time. I've been spending more time out here. As long as I'm in the area, I figured I could take a dog along with me."

"Great—Jazz is getting a little bored with me," Chad said.

"Is she still here?"

"She sure is. Like I told you, older dogs aren't in big demand."

"Oh, the poor thing—I never imagined that she'd still be here. Of course, I'll be happy to walk her. I think she needs a friend," Heidi offered.

"Well, first things first. You have to fill out some paperwork and get approved before you can work with the animals in the rescue," Chad pointed out. "Here, let me find an application."

She followed him to a makeshift desk in the front of the store, where he pushed aside and shuffled papers. "I'm sorry. I know there's an application in here somewhere," he apologized. "It's just that we're planning a fundraiser, and I'm kind of swamped with finding a venue and entertainment, vendors and …"

"Vendors? Will you be serving food?" Heidi asked.

"Yes, but we can't afford the minimum that some places require. I'm having difficulty trying to find a caterer or food service that can accommodate our needs without taking all of our proceeds. It's not easy," he said. "Oh, wait—here it is! I knew there was an application in here somewhere."

Heidi took the application from him and paused, debating if she should speak up. Then she decided it was time.

"Chad, I'm in the planning phase of opening my own food business, and I've been looking for an opportunity to get started. I don't want to put you on the spot, but maybe I could help ..."

"You are? That would be fantastic! Why don't you fill out the app—no, wait. First, tell me about your business. No, wait—"

Laughing, Heidi said, "Actually, there's not a let to tell about the business; it's in the planning phases. But I've been walking around trying to find a venue—I like the thought of catering, and I love the idea of having my own food truck. But there are considerations—like you, I need money. And I can only operate on a part-time basis because I'm not ready to quit my day job. So any investment would have to be limited. There are just lots of considerations."

"I get it. You don't know if it's going to work out yet, so you have to start small. We do the same thing here—volunteers have to be checked. Fosters and adopters have to have home inspections, and even then, everything is done on a trial basis before it's permanent," he said.

"Yes, it's kind of like that. I can't do anything permanent until I know if this is going to work out. And ultimately, the decision will be in the hands of the customers and whether they like my food … or not," she said.

"What kind of food?" asked Chad.

"German cuisine. Authentic German cuisine. Of course, I'd offer some American food—maybe with a little German flair—but my specialties would come from my grandmother's kitchen and the recipes that came from her home country," said Heidi.

"Interesting. And different. I have to admit, I do love a good beer and some kraut," Chad interjected. "So I take it you're a good cook?"

"Some say so—I'd like to think so," Heidi admitted. "Hey, I tell you what, why don't I take this application home and fill it out, and I'll bring it back this weekend with a few items for you to taste?"

"That would be great! I'm here until 6:00 Saturday night. Why don't we set aside an hour or two so we can sit down and work out the details?" Chad suggested.

"It's a date," Heidi said. "Tell Jazzy not to go anywhere—I'll be back!"

* * *

When she returned that weekend, Chad gave her a cook's best compliment—a fantastic appetite. Judging by the fact that he ate everything she brought, he truly enjoyed the food she'd prepared.

"If you want my review, I give it five stars!" he exclaimed. "You're hired!"

After he ate, they talked about the fundraiser. He'd found a venue, one with a commercial kitchen that she would have access to, which was more than she could ask for. After a while, the conversation turned to other requirements of business ownership, and Heidi was surprised to discover that Chad was a great resource. He owned his own business and had experience in such things as licensing, health, inspections, insurance, and personnel—something he reminded her she would need in order to cater an event for approximately 250 people.

"It's not that hard, Heidi. I'll help you. The hiring is easy—you can call a temp service and ask them to provide you with some servers and maybe a line order cook—whatever you need. If you choose not to go with a temp agency, hire a crew on an as-needed basis. That way, if they work out and you need them again, great! If they don't work out, you just don't call on them for other jobs."

"I'm glad you thought of that. Chad, I'm excited, but I have to admit, there are a lot of things to take care of. I've managed other people's businesses before, but not from the ground up. There is a lot to consider, and it can be overwhelming," Heidi said.

"The transition isn't too difficult, Heidi. You've been working in the business sector for a while now. You've been running a department, which in reality isn't all that much different than running your own business. You use the same lessons and training to do both," he pointed out. "The rest of it is universal stuff—the things you can only get from experience, not academics or training."

"I've found that to be true, Chad. That's why I feel so fortunate to have people like John, my mentor, and Mia, my cousin, to share their experience and wisdom with me. And now, there's you—I can already see that I'm going to lean on you for advice and support through this. If you're willing, that is…"

"Of course! Heidi, it's tough taking risks to do what you love—I know, I did it. But I will help you because I know that there is nothing more rewarding than doing what you love and knowing you're making a difference," Chad said.

"The how-to is the hardest part for me, Chad."

"Again, that's not as difficult as it seems, Heidi. You just have to break it into steps and take it one step at a time, even if it's just baby steps. The first step you have to take and can't get around is that you have to visualize your goal. You absolutely have to see your business and your success in your future … before it even happens. I did that when I dreamed of saving animals and giving them a second chance. I actually visualized the rescue before it existed, and I gave myself permission to feel the satisfaction of seeing happy families bring a new pet into their lives. That became my incentive. Whenever I faltered or had doubt, I went right back to that visualization to remind myself why it was worth it and why I was doing the right thing," he explained.

"I think I've done that already, Chad. It took a while— I didn't know if my business was going to be operating from a food truck or somewhere else. I got past that by visualizing being in business in different venues—a food establishment, a pop-up store, and of course, a food truck."

"The other part that must come at the beginning, Heidi, is important. You have to have an absolute expectation that you will make it—you will succeed. If you have any doubt, even the slightest bit, it will provide you with an excuse to give up when things don't go right. Unfortunately, as a business owner, there will always be times when things don't go as planned. It's inevitable," Chad said.

"Thank goodness for John!" Heidi exclaimed. "Believe me, he had his work cut out when he started working with me to increase my confidence! I tip my hat to him, because he managed to make me believe I am capable."

"It's important. Truly, it is. It can make or break even the best business ideas, products, or services. I don't like to talk about it, Heidi, but there are times when I can't help an animal. They're too ill to be saved or have been too abused to acclimate their behavior so they are adoptable. When that happens, I feel defeated and have to fight back doubt that I can make a difference. In those times, I simply want to give up," he admitted sadly.

"I'm sorry, Chad. That can't be easy," Heidi said softly.

"It's okay. It comes with the job. But I do have to remind myself that my successes are greater than my failures, and before I can go out there and do it all again tomorrow, I have to firmly believe that I'm going to succeed. The alternative is not an option in my mind."

"I'll remember that, Chad. So, that's the how to? That's what I need to know?"

"Oh, no, there's more! But those are the two things you have to have to get started. Next, you need to make a plan with a long-term goal and short-term, interim goals that will get you there, one milestone at a time. But let's not put the cart before the horse. First things first, Heidi—visualize your first catering job as a phenomenal success. I know it's not everything you want, but it's a start. You've got to start somewhere … and sometime. Today is a great day to take your first step, and I'll be here by your side to make sure you don't fall," Chad smiled.

Chapter Twelve

YOU CAN'T GO TO BOTH WEDDINGS

The next two months were a whirlwind. Heidi went to work during the day and dedicated her attention to her job and the employees she supervised. She even found some success, and satisfaction, when her department won an internal "rookie of the year award" for having the fastest pace of growth in a new department in the history of the company. There was no time to rest and celebrate, though. Every night and weekend, Heidi was too busy tweaking her menu, finding suppliers and employees for the fundraiser, and meeting with professionals to make sure she had the necessary documentation and protections.

She had to purchase insurance and create an LLC, which would protect her and keep her business separate from her personal finances. There was just so much to entail, but she found that her corporate skills and experience lent themselves to business ownership. She had to understand purchasing and contracts, negotiating skills, and how to communicate with employees and suppliers. Thankfully, she had taken John's advice a couple years before and received her food and sanitation certification, so that was a major hurdle that didn't need to be addressed.

John and Chad were indispensable during the process, and she was more than grateful that she had them to turn to. Their professional opinions and experience were invaluable to her and saved her from making more than one mistake.

But when she started to feel overwhelmed, she turned to Mia, who never failed to give her the encouragement she needed to push through. "Don't worry about perfection—just worry about precision. Be the best you can be and do the best you can do. That's all anyone can do," Mia reminded her. "You've got this! I have faith in you!"

Thankfully, Heidi was too busy on the day of the fundraiser to let anxiety consume her. After checking and double checking, she was certain she hadn't overlooked any details. All she could do now was dive in and hope for the best.

To her relief, everything went relatively smoothly. There were a few glitches, but they weren't major, and Heidi was able to overcome them without any damage. If anything had gone wrong, she was too busy to be able to worry about it, anyway. She was so busy that time flew by quickly. Before she knew it, the food was cleared and the kitchen was clean—her first job was over.

"Chad, how do you think it went?" she asked, anxious for his feedback.

"I heard a lot of compliments on your food, Heidi. I think it was a hit! As a matter of fact, I had to stop what I was doing a few times to give people my caterer's name and number!" he smiled.

"Really?! I'm so relieved. You've helped me so much, I didn't want to let you down, Chad. You don't know how happy I am to hear that," Heidi exclaimed.

"You didn't let me down. Everything was a success, Heidi. In fact, we raised more money in this fundraiser than we ever have. It's been a great night, but I know you must be exhausted. Why don't you go home and get some rest? I'll give you a call in the morning," he said.

"I think I'm too excited to sleep, but you're right— besides, I need to get home to Jazzy. She's starting to get a little separation anxiety when I leave her too long," she laughed.

During the course of the past couple months, Chad and Heidi had frequently worked together, so much so that Heidi finally caved and took Jazz home. Initially, she claimed she was only going to foster her until she got a permanent home, but Chad knew they were a perfect fit and Jazz had found her forever home. One of these days, he told himself, he was going to get Heidi to make the adoption official.

Heidi and Chad had grown closer, too. They found themselves calling each other for coffee or to grab a sandwich, even when they weren't working on the fundraiser. She frequently popped in on the weekend, lunch basket in hand, and they'd each grab a leash and a dog and enjoy an hour together at the park. Now that the fundraiser was over, it was only natural that Chad would call her. They had developed a mutual admiration and friendship — and Chad was interested in seeing if it could lead to a more meaningful relationship in the future.

John picked up on it, too.

In their next meeting, Heidi was telling her mentor that her first catering job was a success. He could hear the excitement in her voice as she reiterated the events of the busy day and those leading up to it, but it was when she brought Chad into the conversation that he could see that same excitement in her eyes. John kept his observation silent; he'd learned long before that things often worked out for the best when no one intervened. Besides, this was personal, and unless Heidi asked for advice, it wasn't his job to offer it.

When Heidi informed him that she had already received a phone call from another potential client, he turned the conversation to other areas, specifically planning and profits.

John explained that she had to predetermine how many jobs she wanted to accept—how much could she take on without taking on too much? Just one job a weekend ... or could she possibly do more? Did she want to start out small and grow over time? If so, how much time and how much growth? What was the long-term goal ... and what were the interim goals that she needed to achieve along the way?

Then, he addressed pricing and profits, reminding her that it was great to quote affordable rates, but she was taking the risk and the financial liability. She deserved a reasonable income, which meant profits were necessary, especially if she wanted to reinvest anything in the business. Again, they were tough questions, but John helped her create a plan that was reasonable and achievable.

About four months later, Heidi informed John that she had been hired to cater a large family reunion in October. The event would take place at one of the family member's homes, which sat on more than five acres—a wooded area that would be beautiful that time of the year. She also noted that it was a perfect time of the year for German fare.

"John, I figured I would set everything up in the pole barn, where they house the farm equipment. It is fully plumbed and has electricity, so I'd have everything I'd need. But when I spoke with the client, I expressed that I wished that I had a food truck. It would really give her family members a fall festival type of flair—how cool would that be?" Heidi said.

"Well, you'll never guess what happened!" she said excitedly. "She said that her uncle used to own a food truck but hadn't used it since he retired. John, she gave him a call, and he said I was welcome to use it! I'm so excited!"

"I can see that, Heidi," John replied. "And this will give you a real taste of what it will be like to have a food truck. It might be a good time to do some preplanning and figure out what you're looking for in a food truck and the features you need—and then what you are willing and able to pay for it."

"You think they'll sell it to me?" she asked.

"I don't know. But I think the time to consider the possibility is now, rather than when you're on the spot and don't think of the details. I will say that I do believe this might be a good opportunity. If it is, I'd say you've reached a milestone in your business. Maybe it's time to apply for that small business loan," he suggested.

* * *

Heidi couldn't believe how fast things were happening. She was able to use the food truck and, with a few adaptations, found it would suit her needs perfectly. She applied for a small business loan and was approved, which gave her the opportunity to participate in festivals and community events, in addition to catering. Within a few months, she encountered her first major business problem—she had to turn down a potential job.

"John, for the very first time, I had to say no to a customer because I was already booked," Heidi said, sadly.

"Don't be sad—that's a good thing! You're becoming more in demand, Heidi. Unless you're willing and ready to expand and hire another crew, you have to realize you can't be at two places at one time. You can't go to both weddings," he pointed out.

"I know. I just felt terrible having to turn down business. It's a first," Heidi replied.

"Yes, it is. It's a milestone in your business, Heidi. It's also a milestone in your life," said John.

"How so?" she asked.

"Heidi, I think it's time for us to have this conversation. You've been a part-time entrepreneur for nearly a year now, and by all accounts, your business has grown. You're actually turning customers away because you don't have the resources to accommodate them. Maybe it's time for you to make the transition to a full-time entrepreneur," he said.

"You mean it's time for me to submit my resignation here?" she asked, surprised.

"That's exactly what I meant, Heidi. You can't go to both weddings. I think you're at a crossroads and it's time for you to decide which wedding you really want to go to," he smiled.

"Do you think I'm ready?"

"You're ready to fly on your own. I'm sure of it. Go, be the pilot of your life; see where it takes you."

***

It was one of the toughest decisions she'd ever made, but in the end, Heidi knew she was ready to succeed, and ready to fail. Her friend, Emily, wouldn't have agreed, but Heidi didn't consult with her—instead, she had a long talk with Chad, whose opinion had become invaluable to her.

"John is right, Heidi. You can't go to both weddings. You have to pick the one you want to attend, the one where you'll be happiest," he said.

"That's easy—I love being an entrepreneur. I love the flexibility, the freedom I have to mold my business however I want. There's just so much satisfaction in knowing I built it … and the person I'm making successful is me, not someone else," she remarked.

"I'll support you in any way I can, Heidi. I hope you know that," Chad said, reaching for her hand.

"That means a lot to me, Chad. It really does."

"As a matter of fact, I was thinking that it might be time to consider whether you're ready for a partner," Chad said.

"For my business?" Heidi asked, confused.

"For everything, Heidi. As long as you're reaching milestones, I was hoping we could work toward one together. I think an October wedding would be perfect—I happen to know a great caterer. Let's make our dreams come true."

DREAMS ARE THE MOTOR TO YOUR SUCCESS

In order to reach your milestones, you can't give someone else the wheel and sit back, waiting for them to take you where you want to be. You have to be the pilot of your life. But getting behind the wheel and taking control isn't enough—you must take action in order to move in the direction you want to go. You have to gain momentum toward what you want, and your dreams are the most important motor to get you there.

Like Heidi, everyone has a dream. Everyone has goals. However, you need more than goals—you need a why, a strong motive that will keep you moving toward the milestones in your life. It is vital that you understand your motivations so they will keep you focused and committed on your ultimate goal and the impact it will have on your life.

By themselves, every principle and strategy in this book will contribute to your success, bringing you one step closer to the milestones you want to reach. However, when you apply all of the principles in your journey, you will discover that you can make progress at a much faster pace in making your personal and professional dreams a reality.

Achieving your objectives isn't complex, but it does take awareness and focus. While the solutions to the challenges that may come your way might be challenging, they are simple—if you want to achieve your dreams and goals, there are steps that will bring you closer to achieving your milestones. They include:

1. An unwavering belief that everything is possible
2. The will to persevere
3. Overcoming all fear of failure
4. Confidence and faith in yourself, even if everyone says it is not possible
5. The willingness to find and follow your why
6. And a commitment to the process—the how to that will guide you to the life you want.

Let the success principles and strategies take you step by step to the milestones of your own success. The sooner you begin, the sooner you'll find yourself saying:

"I may not be where I want to be,
but I'm closer than I was yesterday."

Dr. Greg Reid

PETER BRANDL

The ultimate CEO co-pilot! What use are the best stories, if they are not transferable to everyday work? Peter Brandl connects the worlds in which he is at home: aviation and management – professional pilot and flight instructor but also entrepreneur and management consultant. With over 3,000 events in 23 countries, he is one of the most experienced speakers in the market. Furthermore, he has founded several companies and has been a consultant and sparring partner for top managers of various companies for more than 20 years.

To learn more, visit www.peterbrandl.com.

Also by Peter Brandl:

Crash Communication – Management techniques from the cockpit to maximize performance

(Morgan James Publishing, 2016)

KATJA PORSCH

Katja Porsch is one of the most successful motivational speakers in the German-speaking world. She is the "Do Queen," who empowers people to become the DOer of their life. She is the founder of the "DOer University," the co-founder of Carinthia's 1st Start-up Academy, author of five books, a sought-after expert in the media, and much more. According to Katja, the difference in dreaming and achieving is doing.

She knows success never happens due to favorable circumstances. "I can imagine better starting conditions than two bankruptcies. How I dealt with these circumstances was the deciding factor for my success. The most important thing I have learned in my life is that circumstances are never the reason we fail; it rather all depends on how we deal with them."

To learn more, visit www.katja-porsch.com.

About the Author

DR. GREG REID

Bestselling author, acclaimed speaker, master storyteller, and filmmaker, Greg Reid is a natural entrepreneur known for his giving spirit and a knack for translating complicated situations into simple, digestible concepts. As an action-taking phenomenon, strategy turns into fast and furious results, and relationships are deep and rich in the space he orbits.

Published in over 100 books, 32 bestsellers, 5 motion pictures, and featured in countless magazines, Greg shares that the most valuable lessons we learn are also the easiest ones to apply. Besides being chosen as a Top 10 Speaker by Forbes/Inc/Entrepreneur, Greg has been hand selected by The Napoleon Hill Foundation to help carry on the teachings found in the bible of personal achievement, *Think and Grow Rich*. His latest movie, *Wish Man*, features the life story of Frank Shankwitz (co-founder of the Make A Wish Foundation).

GregReid.com
WishManMovie.com

www.ingramcontent.com/pod-product-compliance
Lightning Source LLC
Chambersburg PA
CBHW072128090426
42739CB00012B/3105